Feminist Ecocriticism

Ecocritical Theory and Practice

Series Editor: Douglas A. Vakoch, California Institute of Integral Studies, USA

Ecocritical Theory and Practice highlights innovative scholarship at the interface of literary/cultural studies and the environment, seeking to foster an ongoing dialogue between academics and environmental activists. Works that explore environmental issues through literatures, oral traditions, and cultural/media practices around the world are welcome. The series features books by established ecocritics that examine the intersection of theory and practice, including both monographs and edited volumes. Proposals are invited in the range of topics covered by ecocriticism, including but not limited to works informed by cross-cultural and transnational approaches; postcolonial studies; ecofeminism; ecospirituality, ecotheology, and religious studies; film/media and visual cultural studies; environmental aesthetics and arts; ecopoetics; and animal studies.

Recent Titles

Feminist Ecocriticism: Environment, Women, and Literature, edited by Douglas A. Vakoch

Ecoambiguity, Community, and Development: Toward a Politicized Ecocriticism, edited by Scott Slovic, R. Swarnalatha, and Vidya Sarveswaran

Transversal Ecocritical Praxis: Theoretical Arguments, Literary Analysis, and Cultural Critique, by Patrick D. Murphy

Feminist Ecocriticism

Environment, Women, and Literature

Edited by Douglas A. Vakoch

LEXINGTON BOOKS
Lanham • Boulder • New York • Toronto • Plymouth, UK

Published by Lexington Books
A wholly owned subsidary of Rowman & Littlefield
4501 Forbes Boulevard, Suite 200, Lanham, Maryland 20706
www.rowman.com

10 Thornbury Road, Plymouth PL6 7PP, United Kingdom

Copyright © 2012 by Lexington Books
First paperback edition 2014

British Library Cataloguing in Publication Information Available

Library of Congress Cataloging-in-Publication Data
The hardback edition of this book was previously cataloged by the Library of Congress as follows:

Feminist ecocriticism : environment, women, and literature / edited by Douglas A. Vakoch.
p. cm.
1. Ecofeminism in literature. 2. Ecocriticism in literature. 3. Feminist literary criticism. 4. Nature in
literature. 5. Ecology in literature. 6. Human ecology in literature. 7. Feminism and literature—
United States. 8. Women and literature—United States. 9. American literature—Women authors—
History and criticism . I. Vakoch, Douglas A.
PS169.E25F46 2012
810.9'355—dc23
2012019104

ISBN: 978-0-7391-7682-5 (cloth : alk. paper)
ISBN: 978-0-7391-9300-6 (pbk. : alk. paper)
ISBN: 978-0-7391-7683-2 (electronic)

♾™ The paper used in this publication meets the minimum requirements of American
National Standard for Information Sciences Permanence of Paper for Printed Library
Materials, ANSI/NISO Z39.48-1992.

Printed in the United States of America

To Joe Subbiondo, for fostering innovative scholarship across disciplines.

Contents

Acknowledgments

I thank the authors of the chapters that follow—Vicky Adams, Monique LaRocque, Jeff Lockwood, Rick Magee, Eric Otto, Marnie Sullivan, and Theda Wrede—for their innovative contributions in bringing together eco-criticism and feminist literary criticism. I also wish to acknowledge the many scholars who, through their review of drafts of these chapters, have greatly strengthened and focused the final work.

For creating compelling cover art that captures the essence of the book in a visual form, I thank Julie Bayless (www.juliebayless.com).

In my work at the SETI Institute over the years, my colleagues have shared with me their insights about what it takes for civilizations to remain stable over the millennia. This book's focus on environmental issues and sustainability is an outgrowth of those conversations. I especially thank Molly Bentley, Linda Bernardi, John Billingham, Steve Brockbank, Jenny Chynoweth, Edna DeVore, Frank Drake, Sophie Essen, Andrew Fraknoi, John Gertz, Gerry Harp, Gail Jacobs, Jane Jordan, Ly Ly, Chris Neller, Tom Pierson, Karen Randall, Jon Richards, John Ross, Pierre Schwob, Seth Shostak, and Jill Tarter.

More recently, I warmly acknowledge the administration, faculty, staff, and students of the California Institute of Integral Studies (CIIS), especially for support from Joseph Subbiondo, Judie Wexler, and Tanya Wilkinson. The work of editing this volume was made possible through a generous sabbatical leave from my other academic responsibilities at CIIS in the spring of 2012. In addition, I thank Harry and Joyce Letaw, as well as Jamie Baswell, for their support of this work.

I am indebted to Justin Race for shepherding the book through the editorial process at Lexington Books. Sabah Ghulamali has my gratitude for helping to move the book swiftly and efficiently into production. I deeply appreciate Lindsey Porambo's steadfast guidance and support in publishing the paperback edition of this book, as well as her ongoing leadership in developing Lexington Books' Ecocritical Theory and Practice series. Finally, I thank Stephanie Brooks for conscientiously overseeing all aspects of the production process, as the final manuscript was transformed into the published volume you are now reading.

Douglas A. Vakoch
San Francisco and Mountain View, California

Introduction

A Different Story

Douglas A. Vakoch

The essence of feminist literary criticism is difficult, if not impossible, to define. In part, the challenge arises from the many ways the term is used.[1] In the context of studying literature, some use "feminist criticism" to refer to any criticism written by a woman, regardless of the subject matter. Others restrict the use to criticism written by women from a specifically feminist perspective, whether the original work being analyzed was written by a woman or a man (Kolodny 1975b). Still others would make the term inclusive enough to refer to literary criticism written by either women or men, as long as the analysis is informed by feminism.

Feminist criticism also resists generalization in terms of its methods and ultimate goals. Instead, it recognizes as legitimate a plurality of approaches—sometimes even in contradiction to one another (Rooney 2006). Critics have often viewed these sometimes incompatible strategies with caution, reflecting a lack of coherence and clear definition. In contrast, others have argued that such pluralism in feminist literary criticism is the only stance consistent with the multiple ideologies that inform the broader women's movement, and that a quest for a uniform conceptual model is antithetical to the enterprise. While for some this pluralism portends a chaotic future for literary inquiry, others argue that by embracing such pluralism, feminists can continue to search even more deeply for patterns of oppression as well as connection. To acknowledge the value of multiple perspectives, they must merely forfeit the claim that their current theories are self-sufficient and all-encompassing (Kolodny 1980/2007).

Similarly, ecocriticism has multiple manifestations. Stated succinctly, ecocriticism examines the relationship between the physical environment and literature (Glotfelty 1996). Some ecocritics, however, avoid an overarching description that is universally applicable, seeing their field instead as a confluence of practices in which diversity of approach is a virtue. But regardless of the theoretical or methodological stance from which they begin, ecocritics are committed to keeping environmental issues at the center of their work (Buell 2005).

The openness of both feminist literary criticism and ecocriticism to multiple, even incompatible perspectives, without the insistence on unitary definitions of their fields, provides the possibility for the formation of a new field: feminist ecocriticism. This hybrid discipline is also called ecofeminist literary criticism, which has been described as "politically engaged discourse that analyzes conceptual connections between the manipulation of women and the nonhuman" (Buell, Heise, and Thornber 2011: 425).[2]

This cross-fertilization of perspectives has already begun to make itself apparent, with ecofeminism being seen as one of the catalysts for ecocriticism's increasing recognition of the complexity of environmental issues. Like feminist theory, ecocriticism recognizes the discontinuities and tensions between historical and poststructuralist approaches to its discipline, as well as between Western perspectives and more globally inclusive understandings. Ecocriticism has increasingly acknowledged the complex interplay of environment and culture, and feminist perspectives have provided a guide for doing so (Buell 2005).

In the years immediately following François d'Eaubonne's coining of the word "ecofeminism" (d'Eaubonne 1974), few literary critics adopted this perspective. Nevertheless, related ideas were being discussed in other areas of the humanities and social sciences. For example, anthropologist Sherry B. Ortner (1974) argued that the universal devaluation of women relative to men could be explained by assuming that women are seen as being closer to nature than men, while men are seen as being more intimately connected with the "higher" realm of culture (Vakoch 2011). But in literature departments, the intersections of ecology and feminism were largely ignored during the 1970s and 1980s (Gaard and Murphy 1998). By the following decade, however, literary critics had begun to examine in depth "'the woman/nature analogy,' defined by Warren as 'the connections—historical, empirical, conceptual, theoretical, symbolic, and experiential—between the domination of women and the domination of nature'" (Carr 2000: 16). Though the significance of a specifically ecofeminist perspective for ecocriticism has been recognized by some, its potential has largely been seen as unfulfilled (Garrard 2004).

ANOTHER STORY

It is the story that makes the difference. It is the story that hid my humanity
from me, the story the mammoth hunters told about bashing, thrusting, raping,
killing, about the Hero. . . .
  It sometimes seems that that story is approaching its end. Lest there be no
more telling of stories at all, some of us out here in the wild oats, amid the
alien corn, think we'd better start telling another one, which maybe people can
go on with when the old one's finished. Maybe.
Ursula K. Le Guin, "The Carrier Bag Theory of Fiction" (1989: 168)

Earlier collections on ecofeminist literary criticism (Gaard and Murphy
1998; Carr 2000; Campbell 2008) have provided examples of literature that
reveal the oppressiveness of patriarchal, dualistic thinking. The current volume builds upon these works to explore the range of specifically *emancipatory* strategies employed by ecofeminist literary critics as antidotes, asking
what our lives might be like as those strategies become increasingly successful in overcoming oppression. In this view, ecofeminism should not be confined to critique, but should instead identify and articulate liberatory ideals
that can be actualized in the real world, in the process transforming everyday
life (Carr 2000). In the process of exploring literature from ecofeminist perspectives, we can expect to reveal strategies of emancipation that have already begun to give rise to more hopeful ecological narratives (Murphy
1991).

  For example, by Douglas Werden's (2001) ecofeminist analysis, Edna
Ferber's novel *So Big* challenges dualism by advancing an ideal of beauty
that repudiates patriarchal preconceptions. As Werden recounts the life of
Selina DeJong, a woman farmer who is the protagonist of this early twentieth-century work, at the outset of the novel we see the link between the male
domination of the land and the domination of women. On a personal level,
this is manifest in the relationship between Selina and her husband; on a
broader societal level, it is evident in the expansion of capitalist agribusiness.

  The dual oppression of women and nature is symbolized in *So Big* by
Selina's future husband picking a trillium flower, taken from a neighboring
man's woods. Once this flower is picked, along with the three life-giving
leaves nestled immediately below it, the plant is destined to die or take years
to recover. So too is Selina's exuberance for life threatened by her husband's
dismissiveness, domination, and neglect—attitudes and actions that are reflected more broadly in his farming practices.

  In *So Big*, we see how Selina benefits by caring for the land and the
farm's animals, employing conservation methods long before they were
common practice. Initially, she benefits slowly, continually constrained by
her husband's opposition to improvements. After his death, however, she
prospers. Supporting her son's college education by diversifying and expand-

ing her farming operation, Selina overcomes dualistic thinking, with the abundance of her farm yielding both financial and spiritual sustenance. Similarly, she values individuals who live in urban environments, as well as in rural settings—not falling prey to a simplistic urban/rural dichotomy of valuation. In the process, tapping a multiculturalism espoused by many ecofeminists, Selina revels in coming to know and care for people of diverse ethnic and socioeconomic backgrounds.

Selina cultivates beauty through her relationship with the land—symbolized through the elegance of her weathered hands. Not bound by patriarchal notions of feminine pulchritude, she redefines beauty in a way that ultimately reflects the richness of her own life as she engages with others, not avoids them. To Selina, beauty is "all the worth-while things in life. All mixed up. Rooms in candle-light. Leisure. Colour. Travel. Books. Music. Pictures. People—all kinds of people. Work that you love. And growth—growth and watching people grow. Feeling very strongly about things and then developing that feeling to—to make something fine come of it" (Ferber 1923: 209; as cited in Werden 2001: 195). As Werden observes, Selina embodies the core principles of ecofeminism nearly a half century before the movement was formally recognized.

ON THE VARIETIES OF ECOFEMINISM: THE RELATIONSHIP BETWEEN WOMEN AND NATURE

This volume's opening chapter, Eric Otto's "Ecofeminist Theories of Liberation in the Science Fiction of Sally Miller Gearhart, Ursula K. Le Guin, and Joan Slonczewski," helps us understand a panoply of ways that women and nature might relate to one another. In his analysis of Gearhart's (1979) *The Wanderground: Stories of the Hill Women*, Le Guin's (1985) *Always Coming Home*, and Slonczewski's (1986) *A Door Into Ocean*, Otto distinguishes two stances toward understanding the relationship between women and nature: cultural ecofeminism and rationalist feminism. Throughout this book, we will repeatedly return to these two broad approaches, albeit under varying names.

According to cultural ecofeminism, there is an innate connection between women and nature. By positing an inherent tendency of women to be attuned to nature—to care for it, to recognize their interrelationship with it—cultural ecofeminists recognize the value of actions and characteristics typically devalued by the dominant (patriarchal) culture. But some argue that by identifying these traits as innate, however ecologically positive they may be, the social and historical factors that have led to women's oppression are obscured. Moreover, this essentialist assumption implies that men have inherent limitations in their ability to connect to the natural world by virtue of their sex.

The Wanderground provides a strong statement of cultural ecofeminism through the story of the Hill Women, who have escaped the oppression of patriarchy by establishing a civilization in the wild based on pacifism, receptivity, and interconnectedness. Possessing spiritual capacities that could not emerge in the presence of men, the Hill Women are connected to one another and to nature in a manner unknowable to men from the City.

Ultimately, Otto concludes, Gearhart's depiction of maleness and femaleness in *The Wanderground* is essentialist, positing unchangeable tendencies. While there are moments when she opens the possibility of an alternative to this dualistic depiction of the sexes, she ends by reaffirming the dichotomy. For example, she describes a band of men known as the Gentles, who recognize that the planet's hope lies with women; though they have curbed their violent tendencies, the Gentles recognize their latent aggressiveness and remain separate from women.

While *The Wanderground, Always Coming Home*, and *A Door Into Ocean* all articulate aspects of cultural ecofeminism, the latter two especially also include elements of rationalist feminism, which is "grounded in the potentiality of human beings to consciously and rationally create a free ecological society" (Biehl 1991: 130; cited by Otto). In the process, *Always Coming Home* and *A Door Into Ocean* expose the tensions that ecofeminist theorists and practitioners confront as they attempt to challenge the oppression of women and nature.

Le Guin's *Always Coming Home* clearly articulates the oppressiveness of her future world's masculine Condor society, living in a post-Industrial Age "City of Man" that, like its predecessor civilization, exists "outside the world" (Le Guin 1985: 153; cited by Otto). The male Condor warriors strive to be united with "the One" through denunciation of the rest of existence, "killing the world, so that they could remain perfectly pure" (Le Guin 1985: 201; cited by Otto), believing "that animals and women were contemptible and unimportant" (Le Guin 1985: 345; cited by Otto). In contrast, *Always Coming Home*'s matriarchal Kesh society offers liberation through an intermingling of human and nonhuman natures. The ecological interconnectedness of life and the rest of nature is reflected in the Kesh's typology of entities, highlighting the kinship of the heavens and the earth, as well as humans, animals, and plants.

But LeGuin's novel does not reflect an essentialist stance. The Condor patriarchy is portrayed as being more malleable than biologically determined, conditioned by its hierarchical religious language. Similarly, the ecological sensibilities of the Kesh reflect the influence of egalitarian language and inclusive rituals more than inherent feminine attributes. Consistent with rationalist feminism, Le Guin suggests the possibility of overcoming oppression by restructuring social practices.

Finally, Otto considers Slonczewski's *A Door Into Ocean*, which describes the response of the all-female waterworld of the Sharers when threatened by the patriarchal forces of a neighboring planet. In the same way the Condor are likened to their Industrial Age precursors in Le Guin's *Always Coming Home*, the patriarchy in Slonczewski's novel is compared to an earlier civilization that destroyed itself in a nuclear holocaust. The common lesson from these ancestral examples is that a world can hope to sustain itself only by moving beyond hierarchical domination. In *A Door Into Ocean*, this awareness of the oppressiveness of hierarchy extends beyond a repudiation of patriarchy, and also encompasses a critique of racial essentialism and anthropocentrism. So too is sexual essentialism challenged. The notion that either sex has a fixed range of responses is contested by examples: the brutally aggressive Chief of Staff of the patriarchal army is female, while a male teenager from the same dominating society willingly finds a new home in the egalitarian world of the Sharers.

FOSTERING EMANCIPATORY ALTERNATIVES

In the next three chapters, we move to an examination of the *preconditions* for instantiating and communicating ecofeminist alternatives. Theda Wrede's "Barbara Kingsolver's *Animal Dreams*: Ecofeminist Subversion of Western Myth" shows the importance of relationality for fostering egalitarian alternatives. The heroine of Kingsolver's (1990a) *Animal Dreams*, Codi Nolina, learns how to inhabit the town in which she was born by caring for members of her community. Avoiding an essentialist dichotomy that would preclude men from developing such a sense of relationality, Wrede suggests that men are more impeded by a cultural script that advocates individualism than by an inherent incapacity for intersubjectivity.

Drawing on Jessica Benjamin's (1988) psychoanalytically-based model, Wrede emphasizes the value of developmental notions drawn from the object relations school. Rather than viewing maturity as arising from the eventual separation from the mother, as did Freud, Benjamin emphasizes the value of the close early maternal bond in developing a sense of intersubjectivity. In this model, autonomy does not arise from separation, but from "mutual recognition," in which successful individuation depends on parents' ability to navigate their children's attempts to control them. Depending on the expectations of the culture in which they are reared, boys and girls can develop a sense of self in starkly different ways. Boys may feel the demand to become autonomous, resulting in a sense of emptiness, while girls may lose their sense of self by merging with their mothers. While excessive domination or submission may interfere with mutual relationships with others, an adequate level of reciprocity can yield a "paradoxical mixture of otherness and togetherness" (Benjamin 1988: 14–15; cited by Wrede).

When Wrede uses these ideas to analyze Kingsolver's (1990a) *Animal Dreams*, we see the protagonist, Codi, develop a strong sense of interrelationship with both her community and the land. Having lost her mother as a young girl, Codi is initially unable to engage in meaningful relationships with others. By shifting her focus from herself to her community's environmental problems, however, she develops a capacity to care. This care is not a form of self-sacrifice, however, but involves reciprocal responsibilities and rewards. Through an increased engagement in environmental activism, Codi fosters a more sustainable physical environment, while also increasing her ability to rely upon a culturally diverse community.

* * *

A decade later, Kingsolver (2000) returns to related themes in her novel *Prodigal Summer*, as Richard M. Magee demonstrates in "Reintegrating Human and Nature: Modern Sentimental Ecology in Rachel Carson and Barbara Kingsolver." Each of the three intertwined plots of *Prodigal Summer* recounts the conflict between an ecologically minded woman and an anti-environmental man, with the three plots intersecting through family ties and bonds within a single rural community. In each case, the women are "arcadian ecologists," individuals who are not reliant solely or even primarily on scientific reason and causal explanation in understanding the environment, but who instead emphasize an empathetic understanding of the natural world.

The interconnection between human action and environmental response is clear throughout *Prodigal Summer*. The ubiquity of cockleburs, plants seen as a nuisance to local farmers, is ultimately traced back to the actions of an earlier generation of settlers, who overhunted the parakeets that had consumed these plants. With the incursion of humans, and their appetite for the birds, the delicate balance of the ecosystem was disrupted.

Kingsolver's *Prodigal Summer* compellingly conveys the interdependence of humans and the environment through a narrative that is emotionally charged while simultaneously being scientifically accurate. A similar rhetorical strategy, Magee notes, is used by Rachel Carson (1962) in *Silent Spring*. As only one example, when Carson recounts the poisoning of a one-year-old child with an insecticide—originally reported in a medical journal—she repeatedly refers to the infant as a "baby," capturing the image of a Christ-child, innocent but taking on the sins of those who were guilty of using this toxic chemical. Both Kingsolver and Carson, trained as scientists but not limited to the language of reductionistic science, communicate environmental threats in an emotionally immediate manner, while portraying nature as intimately related to human communities.

* * *

Repeatedly in this volume we encounter the problems presented by dualistic thinking, manifested in a range of dichotomies, especially male versus female and human versus nature. As we seek to overcome these dichotomies, to avoid living in only half of realities that can be characterized by two poles, we can learn much from those who have traveled through boundaries of nature and culture. As Charles S. Brown (2007, x) notes, "[P]roblems of boundary formation and negotiation recur at all levels, and a coming to an understanding of the nature and types of boundaries poses a truly interdisciplinary challenge to environmental thinkers."

Marnie M. Sullivan's "Shifting Subjects and Marginal Worlds: Revealing the Radical in Rachel Carson's Three Sea Books" provides insights into border-crossing that help us understand both the possibilities and threats of living and thinking at the margins between realms. In *Under the Sea-Wind*, *The Sea Around Us*, and *The Edge of the Sea*, all written over two decades before the same author's better-known *Silent Spring* appeared, Carson shows the reader "that human beings are no longer of central importance" by examining the life within the boundary "where sea meets land, where life emerged from the sea in the course of its leisurely evolution" (Gartner 1983: 69; cited by Sullivan).

As Sullivan explains, Carson continually reminds us that boundaries may not be obvious. The edge of a land mass and the beginning of an ocean may be obscured; a continental shelf may extend outward far into the water, invisible to the human eye at the ocean's surface. Similarly, the ocean below is far from homogeneous. Its varied life is distributed in horizontal strata, each layer a distinct bioregion, an ecosystem of interrelated species.

While the transgression of boundaries can be invigorating, as seen in geographical regions where human cultures meet, it can also be dangerous. As Carson (1951/1989) observes in *The Sea Around Us*, a feeding fish that wanders too far above its habitual life zone may be afflicted with the bends; the lowered pressure of the higher stratum expands the gas within the fish's air bladder, pushing the animal ever nearer the surface. If the fish cannot force itself downward quickly enough, such a boundary crossing may be fatal. Such lessons from the sea remind us of the threats facing all who would move beyond their habitual environments—dangers with which any theorist or practitioner attempting to avoid constraining dualisms may need to contend.

OUT OF HARMONY

Monique LaRocque's "Decadent Desire: The Dream of Disembodiment in J. K. Huysmans' *A Rebours*" highlights the life-denying consequences of an extreme dualism that sees the male as superior to the female, and culture as superior to nature. The protagonist of J. K. Huysmans' (1884/1969) *A Rebours* (*Against the Grain*), Des Esseintes, is a prototype for the Decadent ideal of seeking refuge from both women and nature, attempting transcendence into a realm of pure aesthetics. This dualism positing the superiority of men over women and of culture over nature has a long history in Western civilizations. LaRocque's chapter reminds us that this dichotomy is expressed even more clearly during certain historical periods and in specific artistic schools, such as the late nineteenth-century Decadent movement that was, in part, a response to Romanticism's valorization of unbridled nature.

The particular life history of Des Esseintes contributes to his starkly dualistic repudiation of nature and women. The death of his mother while he was a young child deprived him of a sense of relationality, an important factor in one's capacity to develop a more egalitarian and non-dominating relationship with nature—an idea highlighted in Wrede's chapter exploring the development of a sense of connectedness to others in early childhood.

For Des Esseintes, nature is at its best—and safest—when it is controlled and distanced. This is seen in his description of the terrain as viewed from his window, high upon a hilltop. From that vantage point, he looks outward and downward, seeing the remote landscape as if it were a mere representation in a painting and not part of the natural environment. In parallel, Des Esseintes seeks refuge from his body by devaluing his sexuality—hosting a dinner to celebrate his impotence—which also allows him to escape the threats posed by women, reminiscent of the Gentles' withdrawal from women in *The Wanderground*.

But we should not view Des Esseintes, LaRocque argues, as simply a pathological individual, but rather as a manifestation of late nineteenth-century capitalism. In Des Esseintes' eyes, women are like the material objects created to satisfy the needs of consumers. He sees women as monotonously the same, like mass-produced trinkets or wind-up machines. Through this denigration of women, coupling the individual tendencies of Des Esseintes with the economic forces of his society, we see the life-denying consequences of a dualistic, hierarchical mindset that valorizes the masculine and the aesthetic over the feminine and the natural.

* * *

Vicky L. Adams observes in "'Discourse Excellent Music': Romantic Rhetoric and Ecofeminism in Mary Shelley's *The Last Man*" that the recognition of agency within nature is consistent with contemporary ecological theories founded on chaos and complexity. Adams affirms Carolyn Merchant's (2003: 216–217; cited by Adams) call for seeing nature as "an active subject, not a passive object," rather than viewing the forces of nature in stable balance, as posited by those relating to nature in egocentric, as well as social-interest and ecocentric ethical frameworks. Merchant suggests we consider ecologist Daniel Botkin's (1990) metaphor of "discordant harmonies." Botkin states that the harmony of nature is reflected not in simple, invariably pleasant melodies but through contrasting passages of strife and resolution. A capacity to hold the tension between such opposites, Adams argues, helps us confront environmental challenges in their full complexity.

Adams finds these competing ethics in Shelley's *The Last Man*, a Romantic era future history, set in the late twenty-first century and narrated through the recollections of the last survivor of ecological disaster. Shelley portrays the disastrous effects that pride and personal ambition can have on the environment and in turn on humankind, ultimately leading to the plague spreading to all nations. In one scene, Lord Raymond (the Byronic character) sets the tone of discourse when he favorably recounts those philosophers who "have called man a microcosm of nature, and find a reflection in the internal mind for all this machinery visibly at work around us"; and he goes on to quote Francis Bacon's observation that "the falling from a discord to a concord, which maketh great sweetness in music, hath an agreement with the affections, which are re-integrated to the better after some dislikes" (Shelley 1826/1996: 54, cited by Adams). Yet strong individual desires defeat Raymond's best intentions, just as Bacon's project to exert dominion over nature and Descartes' mechanistic dualism have unexpected consequences. Adams warns against searching for a more harmonious relationship between nature and society through a simple merging of opposites, advising instead that contrary voices be "carefully composed in order to allow for difference without cognitive dissonance."

EMBRACING CONTRADICTION

As Lee Quinby (1990: 126) observes, to embrace seemingly contradictory views can be challenging, even for avowed ecofeminists: "Like the ecology and feminist movements from which it derives, ecofeminism is not devoid of impulses to develop a 'coherent' theory." And yet, Quinby argues, such an emphasis on coherence and consistency is limited in the face of modern power relations through which domination occurs. By Quinby's (1990: 123) analysis, ecofeminism is most effective in opposing the oppressions of modern power by maintaining a multiplicity of theories and practices: "Against such power, coherence in theory and centralization of practice make a social movement irrelevant or, worse, vulnerable, or—even more dangerous—participatory with the forces of domination."

In this spirit of embracing seemingly contradictory positions, Jeffrey A. Lockwood considers the dangers of excessive coherence for ecofeminism in his afterword. In "Ecofeminism: The Ironic Philosophy," he observes that "an element of inconsistency seems necessary to live and act in a world where ecological variation, perverse incentives, unintended consequences, moral luck, and humbling complexities abound. And it is in this sense that the ironies arising from the ecofeminists' view of literature might be understood." As Lockwood reviews the preceding chapters, he notes that the contributors to this volume have already made significant progress in moving the field of ecofeminism forward, but that an ongoing ironic stance can help foster deeper self-reflection within this developing discipline.

As examples of the ironies that Lockwood points out, consider his treatment of scientific objectivity, as well as parallels between ecofeminism and other philosophical traditions. In a field that so emphasizes the intimate connectedness between humans and nature, ironically ecofeminists often excel at maintaining a sense of detached objectivity. As Sullivan describes Rachel Carson's suspension of preconceptions to encounter nature in its own terms, we see the sort of detachment that has long been an ideal of scientific practice.

Similarly, in spite of ecofeminists' critiques of prior philosophical systems, we see some striking insights from certain schools of thought. In La-Rocque's chapter, we see the consequences of living one-sidedly in Des Esseintes' unbalanced self-absorption, contrary to Aristotle's emphasis on the virtue of moderation in his *Nicomachean Ethics*. So too can we see parallels between ecofeminism and a more recent philosophical tradition: pragmatism. Both encourage a pluralistic, perspectival understanding of truth, where theory and practice are always intertwined.

CONCLUSION

Ursula K. Le Guin argues in her essay "The Carrier Bag Theory of Fiction" that literature can provide a container for unexplored possibilities—alternatives to the heroic "killer story" of the status quo (1989: 168). In this spirit, this volume examines the interplay of women and environment through a variety of stories, drawing on insights from such diverse fields as chaos theory and psychoanalysis, while examining genres ranging from nineteenth-century sentimental literature to contemporary science fiction. Our aim is to examine the central claim of ecofeminism—that there is a connection between environmental degradation and the subordination of women (Mellor 1997)—with the goal of identifying and fostering liberatory alternatives.

Douglas A. Vakoch

NOTES

1. See Chowdhury (2009) on the heterogeneous meanings of the broader term "feminism."

2. Gaard (2010) suggests that "feminist ecocriticism" and "ecofeminist literary criticism" can be used interchangeably. Bile (2011) and Lockwood (2011) discuss the difficulty of characterizing "ecofeminism" with a single definition.

Chapter One

Ecofeminist Theories of Liberation in the Science Fiction of Sally Miller Gearhart, Ursula K. Le Guin, and Joan Slonczewski[1]

Eric C. Otto

As philosopher Karen J. Warren (2000: 47) argues, male-centered thinking follows a "logic of domination" that promotes the oppositional pair male/female, places a higher value on males in this pair, and as a result justifies inequalities between men and women. The superiority granted to males under this logic excuses the use of social, political, and economic power to subordinate women, and it sanctions a privileged socioeconomic and political stance for men. For Warren and other ecofeminists, the projects of feminism and environmentalism must notice the similarities between this androcentric logic and the cultural logic that constructs a culture/nature opposition, places a higher value on culture, and as a result authorizes human domination over nonhuman nature. Because both feminism and environmentalism are fundamentally critical of domination, each one can find in the other one resources for expanding its attentions and energizing its methods, ultimately to join hands in a coproductive ecofeminism that denounces oppressions of women and nonhuman nature as well as addresses these oppressions with theory and practice. In the words of Greta Gaard (1993: 1), "No attempt to liberate women (or any other oppressed group) will be successful without an equal attempt to liberate nature."

Ecofeminism is a diverse body of critical thought, though, in some forms aligning with deep ecological spirituality and critique of anthropocentrism and in others proposing an emancipatory politics that rejects deep ecology's normative principles. Ecofeminist theorists propose and contest contrary positions. As such, ecofeminism cannot be said to have linked feminism to environmentalism in any consistent or universal way. But this characteristic of ecofeminism does not harm its productiveness as a critical method. In feminist literary scholarship, efforts to negotiate particularly the tension between "affinity" and "constructionist" ecofeminisms have produced some rich results. For example, Karla Armbruster (1998) argues that whether our ecological politics is informed by a perception of an affinity—a kinship or continuity—between women and nature, or by a broader attention to the way differences in race, economic class, ethnicity, gender, and species construct our ideas about human-nonhuman relationships, we will still end up validating the conceptual dualisms and hierarchies that we are critiquing. In the former case the continuity perspective creates "yet another dualism: an uncomplicated opposition between women's perceived unity with nature and male-associated culture's alienation from it" (Armbruster 1998: 98). In the latter case the constructionist "emphasis on differences in gender, race, species, or other aspects of identity can deny the complexity of human and natural identities and lead to the hierarchical ranking of oppressions on the basis of importance or causality" (Armbruster 1998: 98).

I want to follow Armbruster's lead in discovering and fleshing out possibilities for thinking about this long-standing ecofeminist discussion. Methodologically, however, I want to travel down a different path, not because Armbruster's is not clear and fruitful enough. To be sure, her call for ecofeminism to embrace poststructuralist theory in order to resist "recontainment" by dominant dualisms and hierarchies is an invaluable theoretical boundary crossing (Armbruster 1998: 99).[2] And her reading of Ursula K. Le Guin's "Buffalo Gals, Won't You Come Out Tonight" (1987) is equally an invaluable and successful application of her poststructuralist ecofeminism to a work of literature. My effort here is to show how certain works of science fiction read alone or in combination have engaged with central ecofeminist issues at the same time as, and in some cases even before, such issues provoked theoretical deliberations in more academic settings.

As ecofeminist works, Sally Miller Gearhart's *The Wanderground* (1979), Le Guin's *Always Coming Home* (1985), and Joan Slonczewski's *A Door Into Ocean* (1986) envision healthy ecological spaces as the outgrowths of the cultural valuing of the "feminine" and the containment and/or absence of the "masculine"—a move characteristic of affinity ecofeminism. These books narrate affinity, or as I will continue to call it, *cultural* ecofeminist possibility, all portraying women—and societies—who define themselves in ways encouraged by that branch of ecofeminism: against the dominant logic of patriarchy and through their own personal and local experiences, through collective histories, and/or through Earth-based spiritual traditions. But these texts do not represent exclusive, uncontested cultural ecofeminist positions. They balance and at times struggle with their cultural ecofeminist ideas and other ecofeminist positions. For this reason, Gearhart's, Le Guin's, and Slonczewski's works perform within and among their narratives the critical dialogue important for ecofeminist theory then—in the formative years of ecofeminism (the late 1970s through the 1980s)—and even now, when such discussions remain pedagogically and politically important. They stage within their fictions the very debate that ecofeminism grapples with as a transformative environmentalist movement searching for ways to challenge the oppressions of women and nonhuman nature effectively, and to perform this challenge while maintaining the best theoretical and practical work of ecofeminism's many iterations.

THEORIES OF LIBERATION

Sherry B. Ortner (1974) establishes a context for discussing the differences between cultural ecofeminism and more constructionist, rationalist ecofeminisms. An anthropologist, Ortner finds men's subordination of women to be universal and asks what it is in every culture that leads to this subordination. She reasons that the pancultural oppression of women follows from the likewise pancultural tendency to identify women with nonhuman nature. Ortner borrows from Simone de Beauvoir to show that breasts, the uterus, menstruation, and pregnancy highlight humanity's fundamental animality, our inescapable belonging to the class Mammalia. Since *culture*, by definition, values human engagement "in the process of generating and sustaining systems of meaningful forms (symbols, artifacts, etc.) by means of which humanity transcends the givens of natural existence," patriarchy emerges as culture's defense against whatever would remind civilization of humanity's inability to fully realize this transcendence, including the menstruating and lactating female (Ortner 1974: 40). Women are thus forced into the home, where they can exercise their "natural" roles as mothers to animal-like infants that are "utterly unsocialized," "unable to walk upright," and unfamiliar with social language (Ortner 1974: 45-46). "[W]oman's body," Ortner concludes, "seems to doom her to mere reproduction of life" (Ortner 1974: 43). On the other hand, "the male . . . lacking natural creative functions, must (or has the opportunity to) assert his creativity externally, 'artificially,' through the medium of technology and symbols. In so doing, he creates relatively lasting, eternal, transcendent objects, while the woman creates only perishables—human beings" (Ortner 1974: 43). Under the logic of patriarchy, men are the agents of privileged, nonanimal culture; women are of a lower order.

Anthropologist Melissa Leach (1994) is among those who have since critiqued Ortner's argument, mainly because of its claims about the universality of patriarchally constructed woman-nature connections. And without a doubt Leach's analysis of the Mende-speaking people of Western Africa, whose relationships with nonhuman nature disturb any simplified conception of culture as dependent upon oppressing women and nature, does much to dismantle such claims. But as a context for discussing the cultural and rationalist threads of ecofeminist thought, Ortner's research is still useful; for, by highlighting a perceived connection between women and nature, Ortner raises important questions about whether that connection should be welcomed as valuable for social and ecopolitical transformation or challenged as falsely construed and in the end hazardous for feminist and environmentalist projects. Ortner favors the latter, characterizing what Stacy Alaimo (2000: 4) deems "feminist theory's flight from nature."

Drawing from many of the same sources as deep ecology, cultural ecofeminism posits an innate woman-nonhuman nature link and argues that this link should be embraced as a way of dealing with the social and environmental problems inherent and evident in patriarchal culture.[3] Developing in the late 1970s and early 1980s out of radical feminism's repudiation of oppressive social systems and accentuation of ways of knowing and being that contest harsh masculinity, cultural ecofeminism dismantles patriarchy by prioritizing "feminine" values. Cultural ecofeminists "elevate what they consider to be women's virtues—caring, nurturing, interdependence—and reject the individualist, rationalist, and destructive values typically associated with men" (Gruen 1993: 77). Lori Gruen, a critic of cultural ecofeminism, argues that the belief that women and nonhuman nature are connected works to devalue men as unconnected from nature and thus does nothing to restructure the hierarchal relation of privilege that feminism and other social movements have challenged for years. As Val Plumwood (1993: 3) notes, ecofeminists of this "Cavern of Reversal" define their identities "by reversing the valuations of the dominant culture." For cultural ecofeminists, though, the hierarchal relation of privilege is not what is troubling. The direction of the privilege is. Judith Plant (1990: 160) writes as a cultural ecofeminist: "Women's values, centered around life-giving, must be revalued, elevated from their once subordinate role. What women know from experience needs recognition and respect. We have had generations of experience in conciliation, dealing with interpersonal conflicts in daily domestic life. We know how to feel for others because we have practiced it."

Plant does not challenge the validity of the presumption that life-giving, strong interpersonal communication, and empathy are innate to women, which other types of feminism and ecofeminism do challenge by labeling such characteristics as imposed upon women in patriarchal social systems. Her essay in Irene Diamond and Gloria Feman Orenstein's *Reweaving the World* is about what women, specifically, can bring to the bioregionalist project, a project advocating a more life-centered, interpersonal, and connected view of local place. The thought that women are inherently closer to nature and are thus invaluable for the realization of bioregional ways of life is not a problem for cultural ecofeminists. What is a problem is when culture devalues its feminine categories and thus devalues the virtues necessary for a more viable human relationship with nature. While still manifesting hierarchical thinking, cultural ecofeminism argues that privileging care and empathy for all human and nonhuman life, instead of privileging self-interest and the production of marketable goods, are reversals necessary for an ecocentric, life-affirming culture to emerge.

Asserting so-called feminine values is central to Andrée Collard's (1989) ecofeminism, too. Much like Plant, Collard centers her theorizing on the importance for environmentalism of accenting an essential woman-nature connection. She writes, "Ecology is woman-based almost by definition. *Eco* means house, *logos* means word, speech, thought. Thus ecology is the language of the house. Defined more formally, ecology is the study of the interconnectedness between all organisms and their surroundings—the house. As such, it requires a thorough knowledge and an intimate experience of the house" (Collard 1989: 137). As speakers of the language of the house, Collard argues, women endure the domestic burdens relegated to them under patriarchal convention. Women can therefore empathize with the similarly abused nonhuman nature, making them better positioned to address and correct this latter abuse. Relatedly, cultural ecofeminism stresses the need for a collective history of women's oppressions in patriarchy. One project of feminism as a whole is to draw attention to women's history, but the goals of this attention vary. Cultural ecofeminism breaks from the liberal feminist endeavor to achieve equal rights and representation for women using the methods of already existing sociopolitical institutions and instead seeks change by contrasting the modern history of women's oppression with an ancient history allegedly permeated with prepatriarchal ideals such as kinship, egalitarianism, and nurturance. The goal of this juxtaposition is epistemological; lacking knowledge of "what [women] were and therefore what [women] can be . . . encourages women to want incorporation into man's world on an 'equality' basis, meaning that woman absorbs his ideologies, myths, history, etc. and loses all grounding in her own traditions" (Collard 1989: 8).

Much of the work done in cultural ecofeminism involves revaluing matriarchal principles historically documented in archeological studies. In its spiritual forms cultural ecofeminism promotes the reemergence of ancient matriarchal belief systems that coincided in Minoan Crete and Old Europe, for example, with peace and respect for all life. Along with Marija Gimbutas, Riane Eisler, Starhawk (the author of the deep ecological and cultural ecofeminist science fiction book *The Fifth Sacred Thing* [1993]), Charlene Spretnak, Joanna Macy, and Carol P. Christ, Collard is a thinker in this tradition. She and others call on modern culture to embrace or at least adopt some values of Earth-based spiritualities historically seen in Goddess-worshipping cultures. "In cultures where the cycle of life is the underlying metaphor," Starhawk (1989: 175) writes, "religious objects reflect its imagery, showing us women—Goddesses—ripe in pregnancy or giving birth. The vulva and its abstracted form, the triangle, along with breasts, circles, eyes, and spirals, are signs of the sacred." According to Spretnak (1990: 5), many feminists came to ecofeminism after their exposure, through historical and archeological research, to such an ancient religion "that honored the female and seemed to have as its 'good book' nature itself." What was intriguing for early ecofeminists "was the sacred link between the Goddess in her many guises and totemic animals and plants, sacred groves, and womblike caves, in the moon-rhythm blood of menses, the ecstatic dance—the experience of knowing Gaia, her voluptuous contours and fertile plains, her flowing waters that give life, her animal teachers" (Spretnak 1990: 5).

That cultural ecofeminism is caught up in idealism is certainly one of the main criticisms leveled against it. Critics of cultural ecofeminism believe that valuing a woman-nature connection is an ineffective liberatory strategy that fails to dismantle rationally the logics of the social, political, and economic systems responsible for dominations of all types. Susan Prentice (1988) identifies cultural ecofeminism's idealism as its worst characteristic. Advocating an understanding of systems of power and domination more sophisticated than what cultural ecofeminism offers, she writes, "By locating the origin of the domination of women and nature in male consciousness, ecofeminism makes political and economic systems simply derivative of male thinking" (Prentice 1988: 9). For Prentice the assumption that men "think wrong" and that "biology is destiny" "trivializes several centuries of history, economics and politics by simply glancing over the formidable obstacles of social structures" (1988: 9). Janet Biehl (1991) also voices this critique. She chides cultural ecofeminism for narrowly and crudely focusing on patriarchy as *the* cause of oppression, and for assuming that prioritizing women's supposed biologically determined predispositions is a way to eradicate oppression. What about the state, Biehl asks, which historically as an institution has oppressed women, nature, and men alike? Racism is rooted in ethnic chauvinisms and economic motivations unrelated to gender conflict. And capitalism's profit motive and growth imperative have instigated an entire range of oppressions directed at whoever and whatever gets in the way of their realization. Drawing on Prentice's analysis Biehl (1991: 50) concludes, "Systems of domination like capitalism, statism, and ethnic oppressions—and sexism itself—have a 'history, logic, and struggle' of their own"; in no way does elevating women's supposed values above men's supposed values engage the procedures necessary to foster real change.

A strong advocate of rationalist feminism, Biehl also questions the validity of cultural ecofeminism's historical references. Goddess worship does not guarantee a benign culture, she argues, yet cultural ecofeminists seem to honor such worship as "the magic carpet by which we can reclaim the 'women's values' of the Neolithic" (Biehl 1991: 33). Nor does the presence of "full-figured female figurines" in ancient archeological sites confirm that the relative peacefulness of early Neolithic cultures resulted from an embrace and worship of "a generative female principle" (Biehl 1991: 34). The societies of the early Neolithic were complex, and to suggest that their sociopolitical dynamics grew simply out of goddess worship is to ignore the range of social, political, and cultural intricacies that constructed the Neolithic temper. Biehl also references archeological evidence of human sacrifice in Minoan Crete, which suggests a cruelness in that society overlooked in cultural ecofeminism's idealizations.

Biehl (1991: 130) concludes, "With an ecological ethics grounded in the potentiality of human beings to consciously and rationally create a free ecological society, we can begin to develop an ecological political movement that challenges the existing order on the grounds that it denies both humans and nonhumans their full actualization." Biehl's loyalty to reasoned democratic process is crucial, as she values the modes of critical engagement necessary for transformation while at the same time denying legitimacy to gender valuations that would lock women's identities onto eternal, nonnegotiable, and politically feeble concepts of femininity. But as Elizabeth Carlassare (1999: 229) points out, such loyalty comes at the expense of discounting "the work of cultural ecofeminists with their emphasis on transforming consciousness, reclaiming women's history, and fostering a woman-based culture and spirituality." Perhaps there is something valuable not in locating a simple continuity between women and nonhuman nature, but at least in esteeming as a vital part of the ecofeminist dialogue those ideas that have come about as a result of thinkers whose intellectual tendencies move them toward more personal and spiritual transformative modes.[4] As Carlassare (1999: 231) notes, "Criticism of ecofeminism's essentializing tendencies is important to insure critical self-reflexivity and for examining the ways in which essentializing may sometimes work against the goals of women's liberation by homogenizing the diversity of women's experiences. Dismissing cultural ecofeminism on this basis, however, precludes the possibility of learning from this position and obscures the legitimacy of the variety of positions and discursive forms under ecofeminism's umbrella."[5]

THE WANDERGROUND

Published five years after Ortner's anthropological study of patriarchy, and a decade before ecofeminism rose to prominence as a critical perspective in the late 1980s and early 1990s, Gearhart's *The Wanderground* is the story of the Hill Women, an all-female society living nomadically in a wilderness far away from the "City" and its oppressions. Driving the plot is the encroachment of men from the City into the wilderness where, years before, various expressions of male potency—aggressive sexuality, militarism, and destructive technologies—were made impotent by what the Hill Women call both the "Revolt of the Earth" and the "Revolt of the Mother," a juxtaposition of "Earth" and "Mother" characteristic of cultural ecofeminism (Gearhart 1979: 130, 158). Explaining the Revolt, one of the Hill Women says, "Once upon a time . . . there was one rape too many. . . . The earth finally said 'no.' There was no storm, no earthquake, no tidal wave, no specific moment to mark its happening. It only became apparent that it had happened, and that it had happened everywhere" (Gearhart 1979: 158). Guns no longer worked in the wilderness, machines broke down, animals refused to serve men, and the male libido waned. As imagined by Gearhart, this Revolt represents disdain for mythologies of Earth and its processes as tools of a violently retributive god, demonstrating instead Earth as a Gaian female subject peaceably protecting herself against men, who have brought violence upon women, nonhuman animals, and the land. The effects of the Revolt are disappearing, however. Rumors of male virility's return outside the City are leading men to test their sexual strength through acts of rape and group "Cunt Hunts" in the country, generating a fear in the Hill Women that "woman energy might again be drained as it had been for millennia before the Revolt of the Earth" (Gearhart 1979: 160, 130).

The Wanderground supports an inverted masculine/feminine value hierarchy. The novel is self-reflexively aware of its good women/bad men dichotomy, presenting one character, Jacqua, who says to herself early in the book, "It is too simple . . . to condemn them all or to praise all of us" (Gearhart 1979: 2). But right away Jacqua declares, "for the sake of earth and all she holds, that simplicity must be our creed" (Gearhart 1979: 2). This condemnation of men and praise of women is a necessary offensive and defensive mantra for the Hill Women, for their historical experiences do not reveal anything decent in the male sex. In addition, this mantra is key for the novel as a cultural ecofeminist thought experiment and radical feminist speculative text motivated by its historical moment to narrate female subjectivity against patriarchal society's male gaze, as well as to narrate female possibility when released from this gaze's physical and psychological oppressions.

As a result of the Revolt and the subsequent escape of the Hill Women's predecessors to the wilderness, women have been left free to evolve independently of the patriarchal logic of domination. This narrative move facilitates Gearhart's speculation on the qualities inherent in women as free subjects living on what Alaimo (2000: 23) discusses as "undomesticated ground," nature as "a space of feminist possibility." Although to be expected in a science fiction novel bordering on fantasy, these qualities stand out as being more ecological, more embedded and interrelational, than the qualities that the text argues men possess as members of a fundamentally disconnected sex. The Hill Women fly, or "windride." They have a built-in instinctual mechanism called a "lonth" that acts as a flight response allowing involuntary kinesthetic control, demonstrating their return to an animal nature that modernity has sedated. The Hill Women can also communicate telepathically with other Hill Women and with flora and fauna, a phenomenon called "mindstretch" that requires traits associated in cultural ecofeminist thought with the feminine: "Meaningful communication," a Hill Women lesson goes, "is the meeting of two vessels, equally vulnerable, equally receptive, and equally desirous of hearing" (Gearhart 1979: 115). Finally, the Hill Women engage in a ritual called "earthtouch" that uses mindstretching to send energy drawn from Earth by one Hill Woman to another in need of this energy. Combined, mindstretch and earthtouch represent a dynamic, deep ecological, spiritual, and communicative web of interdependencies between one woman and other women, and women and nonhuman nature. This web is an ecological phenomenon permitted to develop as a result of the absence of anti-ecological and enforced patriarchal power.

Just as cultural ecofeminism does more theoretically to elevate what it conceives as women's values than simply to connect women and nature in an essential bond, so too does *The Wanderground* go beyond just conceptualizing women as windriders with more ecologically sound instinctual and communicative awarenesses. The novel also offers up programs for reviewing and challenging modern cultural tendencies that oppress women and nonhuman nature. The apparent essentialism of Gearhart's book thus borders on political possibility, on being "a positive tool of liberation," as Noël Sturgeon (1997: 9) notes of selected essentialist rhetorics. This political possibility ultimately wanes, as I will show below, but the first of these programs motivates ecofeminist practice by uniting the oppressed through their individual histories. Against a destructive patriarchal memory that recalls the potency men used to have outside the City, and thus reinstates the violent misogyny of the past after the effects of the Revolt have worn off, the women of *The Wanderground* stress the importance of a collective and constructive memory that allows members of their liberated society to understand their social history and what motivates their emancipatory project. Thus, while the City continually seeks to impose and perpetuate a master narrative of patriarchal history—requiring every woman to be married, allowing men to have several wives, and instituting curfews on women—the women of the country seek local stories that will illustrate what they are escaping from and to, as well as inform their future. Nowhere in this collective history do the women subscribe to a master narrative of their culture's experience. Instead, "From countless seemingly disconnected episodes the women had pieced together a larger picture so that now they had some sense of what had happened during those last days in the City. Over the years as women had joined them the memory vessels had been added to: more and more stories, more and more horrors, and sometimes a narrative that brought with it some hope or humor. As a woman shared, she became part of all their history" (Gearhart 1979: 23). As a cultural ecofeminist text, then, *The Wanderground* posits competing historical paradigms—one masculine, one feminine—that use historical references either to recreate the social conditions of a predetermined, univocal social system or to create freeing conditions based on an ecology of private experiences.

Second, as the earthtouch ritual shows, the Hill Women are rooted in a deep ecological, Earth-based spirituality that is vital to their selfhood, their kinship, and their sense of place. Indeed, advocating such a spirituality is imperative for cultural ecofeminism. Earthtouch emphasizes what Riane Eisler (1990: 33), a cultural historian, calls a "partnership model of society." Developing out of the Gaia tradition, which regards Earth as "a living system designed to maintain and to nurture life," the partnership model opposes the "dominator society," favoring instead a worldview founded upon ancient spiritualities in which "the world was viewed as the great Mother, a living entity who in both her temporal and spiritual manifestations creates and nurtures all forms of life" (Eisler 1990: 30). Partnership requires empathetic nurturance, and thus from a cultural ecofeminist perspective can only emerge given a revaluing of the feminine. In *The Wanderground*, partnership in earthtouch is exclusive to those whose feminine capacities have been permitted to develop in the absence of masculine power. As a political statement Gearhart's is radically essentialist. To posit a separatist, feminist space where a spiritual ecological conscience can thrive is a key theoretical move for ecofeminist science fiction. As unsophisticated as this move may be, it initiates speculation on what it is in modern cultural cosmology that undermines the human potential for realizing such an ecological conscience: masculine aggression, perhaps, but ideologies of dominance more accurately. So while Gearhart's story "reinforces the exclusivity of the categories of male and female"—something that science fiction scholar Jenny Wolmark (1994: 85) sees as problematical for its adherence to the same old gender assumptions and the resulting failure to question these assumptions—such reinforcement is a viable starting point for an ecofeminist project that endorses a worldview contrary to prevailing dogma.

Rounding out Gearhart's programs for instituting change is *The Wanderground*'s look at the dominant ideology against which the Hill Women elevate their collection of personal histories and their feminine partnership, an ideology embodied by men and their collective space, the technological City. The dystopian City is the institutional space for both men, the oppressors, and technology, the tool of their oppressions. Answering why the Hill Women, with their extraordinary powers, refuse to seek violent revenge on the City with technological weaponry, one Hill Woman insists, "That's the mistake the men made, sisterlove, and made over and over again. Just because it was possible they thought it had to be done. They came near to destroying the earth—and may yet—with that notion" (Gearhart 1979: 145). Thus, the essential quality of men in the novel is being "Driven in their own madness to destroy themselves and us and any living thing" with whatever technology is available (Gearhart 1979: 3). Even using the tool of language, men in the novel impose oppressive standards upon women ("streamlined," "limited," "dependent," "constantly available") (Gearhart 1979: 63).

The Wanderground succeeds as a radical statement of cultural ecofeminism. It establishes and contrasts what it means to be a woman both in the oppressive context of patriarchy and in a liberated context. As women unchained, the Hill Women restore and develop further their innate feminine potentials. Vulnerable, receptive, pacifist, interconnected, wild—these terms describe both the natural world that Gearhart imagines and the women she envisions evolving free from masculine oppressions, women empowered by a Revolt of the Earth-Mother to create themselves as subjects who value the qualities of the feminine traditionally disparaged in patriarchy. To make this empowerment clearer, Gearhart sketches a woman living in the dystopian City as an unmistakably powerless object of the male gaze: "a thickly painted face, lacquerstiffened hair, her body encased in a low-cut tight-fitting dress that terminated at mid-thigh" (Gearhart 1979: 63). This image of stiffness, encasement, and termination reveals the misogyny against which the Hill Women are fighting, a misogyny that permits men to exercise reckless power over women and sustain a civilization of dominance over women and other-than-human nature.

Prefiguring the anti-essentialist insights of Prentice and Biehl, feminist literary critic June Howard (1983: 72) notes of Gearhart's book, "The evaluation of 'feminine' and 'masculine' qualities asserted by radical feminism and by *The Wanderground* . . . lends support to the idea that differences between men and women are 'natural,' and thus endangers the basis of our critique of existing social relations and our belief that they can be changed. The disagreement is between those who accept and build upon the common-sense observation that the sexes differ, and those . . . who argue that gender identity is constructed by complex, socially and historically specific structures." From Howard's point of view *The Wanderground* promises nothing transformative and is actually dangerous in its maintenance of ahistorical gender divisions. To achieve successfully a more fully developed, or at least nuanced, ecofeminism, Gearhart could have further contemplated the simplicity of her novel's universal condemnation of men—the simplicity that her character Jacqua admits. But she passes up this opportunity in favor of cultural ecofeminist polemic. In the novel there exists briefly a potential dissipation of essentialist definitions of men: the book's Gentles are "men who knew that the [Hill Women] were the only hope for the earth's survival" (Gearhart 1979: 2). However, this potential is quickly weakened by a subsequent description of the Gentles as "men who, knowing that maleness touched women only with the accumulated hatred of centuries, touched no women at all" (Gearhart 1979: 2). The Gentles understand their instinctive male aggressiveness and thus choose to abstain from physical contact with women altogether. They know themselves as innately hostile male bodies that require self-policing to ensure the protection of women and nonhuman nature.

Of course, this understanding of the Gentles is Jacqua's, revealed in the passage in which she reflects on and endorses the simplicity of the Hill Women's denunciation of all men. Gearhart's ecofeminist project still shows promise of theoretical complexity, though, when it introduces other Hill Women who question inscribing a predetermined, inborn aggressiveness on the Gentles. Reacting to the developed communicative powers of one of the Gentles, the Hill Woman Betha admits that "her absolutes began to get fuzzy around the edges when she tried to make them apply to a man like Aaron" (Geahart 1979: 115). But again Gearhart does not explore gender difference as more complex than cultural ecofeminism declares. Only women can share power peacefully, her novel insists: "Men—even Gentles—found it difficult or impossible really to share power" (Gearhart 1979: 115). What Betha sees in this Gentle does not instigate a revision of the Hill Women's established beliefs. Rather, his "understanding of the essential fundamental knowledge [that] women and men cannot yet, may not ever, love one another without violence" instead impresses on her a slightly different perception of the Gentles than her perception of men in general (Gearhart 1979: 115). The Gentles are different from the men of the City merely because they realize and contain their natural brutality as well as share the Hill Women's view of human sexual relations.

Gearhart's final opportunity to render a more complex ecofeminism comes when the Hill Women engage with the Gentles in political process. The Gentles have noticed that the increased violence against women outside the City correlates with the number of Hill Women on rotation in the City, and they want to meet with the Hill Women to discuss this trend. As fewer women from the Wanderground make their way in disguise into the City to keep an eye on the conditions there, more abuses against the Hill Women happen in the country. Before the meeting in which the Gentles share this crucial observation, the Hill Women debate whether they should grant the Gentles this meeting at all. Though the meeting does happen, it does not take place without opposition: "To some of the women it did not matter that the gentles were men sworn to isolate themselves from women; if they were men then there was no reason for concourse with them" (Gearhart 1979: 126). But the eventual decision to let several women meet with the men—while unenthusiastic and permitted only under the assurance that the individual women speak only for themselves, not for the group as a whole—signals a step toward a more socially conscious ecofeminism.

In the end, however, the women maintain their essentialism. Their fear of universal masculine aggression prevents them from opening up productive conversation with the Gentles about how both groups can work together to dodge the intruders from the City. Moments after their pledge to communicate the Gentles' observations to other Hill Women, the women return to their separatism after learning that the Gentles have discovered in themselves telepathic powers similar to the Hill Women's. Responding to the Gentles' claim that these powers are nonviolent, Evona says, "Nonviolent? Never. You know what will happen. You'll use your new power all right. You'll use it, perfect it, manufacture it, package it, sell it, and tell the world that it's clean and new because it comes from a different breed of men. But it's just another fancy prick to invade the world with" (Gearhart 1979: 179). Evona's response is laden with the types of ideological barriers that other modes of feminism and ecofeminism avoid in their drives to add more complexity to ecofeminist conversations. The Hill Women's attitude toward the Gentles does not encourage the breakdown of their essentialism into a mode of thought more open to recognizing the potential for anyone, man or woman, to exercise social and ecological consciousness, and thus for progressive social and ecological change to grow out of democratic conversation.

ALWAYS COMING HOME

The Wanderground's brand of ecofeminism defines men as inherently oppressive and liberated women as ecologically conscious. *Always Coming Home*'s ecofeminism is more critical than that, even though Le Guin does reflect several facets of cultural ecofeminist thinking. The Kesh society of her future history interweaves human culture and nonhuman nature in a way that breaks down the culture/nature dualism to favor instead a spirituality of individual, social, and cultural embeddedness in nonhuman nature. This deep ecological, cultural ecofeminist ecospirituality informs the Kesh's social organization and treatment of Earth, as it also combats a patriarchal quest for dominance over nature that would undermine the union with nonhuman nature that the Kesh have achieved. Further, the Kesh's gender identifications are analogous to those of cultural ecofeminism: the Kesh connect "woman and animal . . . throughout [their] sexual and intellectual teaching," an identification that the narrator of this passage declares is *not* used to devalue woman (Le Guin 1985: 420).

Illustrating their spirituality and their gender identifications is a complex symbol, the "heyiya-if." Signifying ecological connection with its dual spirals growing inward, as well as openness to change with its center empty and refusing to finalize that connection, the heyiya-if permeates and defines the Kesh's cultural activities, their dance choreography, stage productions, town planning, art, musical instruments, and meditative practices. The Kesh make "no provision for a relation of ownership between living beings," arranging their society around not just a respect for life—a cultural ecofeminist care ethic—but also a deep ecological sense of their place within the ecosystem (Le Guin 1985: 43). The "Earth People" of the Kesh's "Five Houses of Earth" include "the earth itself, rocks and dirt and geological formations, the moon, all springs, streams and lakes of fresh water, all human beings currently alive, game animals, domestic animals, individual animals, domestic and ground-dwelling birds, and all plants that are gathered, planted, or used by human beings" (Le Guin 1985: 43-44). The "Sky People" of their "Four Houses of the Sky" include "the sun and stars, the oceans, wild animals not hunted as game, all animals, plants, and persons considered as the species rather than as an individual, human beings considered as a tribe, people, or species, all people and beings in dreams, visions, and stories, most kinds of birds, the dead, and the unborn" (Le Guin 1985: 44). Here, Patrick D. Murphy's (2000: 88) thoughts on matrilineal societies are useful: "In matrilineal societies among the first nations, . . . kinship is observed in terms of extended families, lodges, clans, and entire tribes, not nuclear family structures. As a result, it is more accurate to say that there are not others in such cultures, only anothers, that is, beings who are neither self nor other in any absolute dichotomy but are familiar, related, and connected with us."

A specter haunts the ennatured Kesh in the form of a masculinity once prevalent in the aptly named "City of Man"—our own Industrial Age, our now—and now reemerging in the future world of the Kesh in a patriarchally organized warrior group called the Condor, or the Dayao. Representing a time "when [people] lived outside the world," "a sort of peninsula sticking out from the mainland, very thickly built upon, very heavily populated, very obscure, and very far away," the City of Man still exists in the world of *Always Coming Home* in the form of the dangerous industrial toxins modernity left behind (Le Guin 1985: 153). With the Condor this City of Man takes its present form in militaristic aspiration. They want to resurrect the "Great Weapons" of the past, a project identified in Le Guin's book with the essence of masculinity. One weapon, a tank-like vehicle named the "Destroyer," "push[es] through a wall of bricks, thundering and shaking through the ruins it made, huge and blind, with a thick penis-snout" (Le Guin 1985: 349-350). A figurative rape this is, one also extended to the other-than-human world: "The Destroyer push[es] against the oak trees . . . , push[es] them over" (Le Guin 1985: 350). In the masculine culture of the Condor, a "man-dominant" culture, the "identification [of woman and animal] *is* used to devalue" (Le Guin 1985: 420, emphasis added).

Le Guin's book traces one Kesh woman's navigation through this masculine "outside the world" as well as her experiences of living life under the cultural paradigms dominant during the City of Man and now resurfacing as a force against which the Kesh's ecologically conscious Valley culture must struggle. North Owl is the daughter of a woman of a Valley House—Willow—and a man of the oppressive Condor people—Terter Abhao. As one of the Kesh she is among the world as a child enough to recognize "the dirt [as] the mother of [her] mothers" and to make her pre-adolescent ritual one of absolute in(ter)dependence in the wilderness (Le Guin 1985: 19). However, because North Owl's father left the Valley so early in her life to command an army, she has grown up with the title "half-person" (Le Guin 1985: 19). At eight years old she feels incomplete. Terter's return to the Valley with his army prompts North Owl to reflect, "He was home, he was here, our family was whole; now everything was as it should be, balanced, complete; and so it would not change" (Le Guin 1985: 30). But she soon finds out that her fantasies of familial completion, informed by a patriarchal concept of the family, contradict the greater ecological union valued in Kesh culture.

When North Owl leaves the Valley to join her father and experience Condor culture we get a deeper view of this culture's supporting structures, the linguistic, religious, and social configurations that underlie Condor tyranny. In this way, Le Guin's ecofeminism moves away from strict cultural ecofeminist reasoning and into a more critical mode of ecofeminist understanding, one motivated to explore the historically contingent, rather than fixed, features of patriarchy. First, unlike the Kesh's language, the Condor's recognizes hierarchy; Terter renames North Owl "Ayatyu," "woman born above others," while he also refers to the people of other towns as "people of no account" (Le Guin 1985: 186, 189). *Condor* is a hierarchal designation symbolizing people who "go in silence, above all the others" (Le Guin 1985: 189). Second, this linguistic encoding of hierarchy goes hand-in-hand with the patriarchal religion of the Condor people, a monotheism with only one person—a man, "The Condor"—able to interpret the word of "One" (Le Guin 1985: 193). Of religious practice North Owl observes, "Women were not allowed into the sacred parts of their heyimas, which they called *daharda*; we could come no nearer than the vestibule in front of the daharda to listen to the singing inside on certain great festivals. Women have no part in the intellectual life of the Dayao; they are kept in, but left out" (Le Guin 1985: 200). Furthermore, "True Condor warriors were to be one thing only, reflections of One, setting themselves apart from all the rest of existence, washing it from their minds and souls, killing the world, so that they could remain perfectly pure" (Le Guin 1985: 201). And finally, with such language and religion comes an attendant social and familial structure. North Owl narrates, "Certain men belonging to certain families are called True Condors, and others like them are called . . . One-Warriors. No other people are called Condors. Men who are not of those families are all called *tyon*, farmers, and must serve the True Condors. Women of those families are called Condor Women, and must serve Condor men, but may give orders to tyon and hontik. The hontik are all other women, foreigners, and animals" (Le Guin 1985: 193). In contrast to the "anotherness" of which Murphy speaks, the Condor's social reasoning embraces an otherness steeped in a strict division between male warriors—and their approved servants—and "women, foreigners, and animals."

Tied to such linguistic, religious, and social structures, the Condor's masculine oppressiveness loses the ahistoricity and immovability of the masculinity that is represented in *The Wanderground*. The Condor's living "outside the world" is indeed a product of a certain masculinity, but grounded in historically contingent structures, this masculinity is not rigid. That the Condor "believed that animals and women were contemptible and unimportant" and that "Condors' wives were expected to have babies continuously, since that is what One made women for" demonstrates that beliefs and expectations motivate such patriarchal notions (Le Guin 1985: 345). If patriarchy is a sociopolitical construct driven by belief and expectation, then it proves to be far more malleable than if it were biologically defined and, as Gearhart's book largely suggests, inevitable. In the same way, the apparent feminine qualities of Kesh culture are more the product of the pervasive heyiya-if—a linguistic, religious, and social device—than they are of an inevitable feminine principle.

In addition to its content, the form of Le Guin's book draws attention to the artifactual nature of gendered categories. *Always Coming Home* contains excerpts of literature, artwork, maps, and other objects of Kesh and Condor existence. The effect of this cutting and pasting is an emphasis on the constructedness of the Kesh's ecological conscience and the Condor's tyranny, both of which are products of a set of historical relics and not fundamental to sex. The heyiya-if produces and is produced by the ecological mindset of the Kesh just as the Condor's crimes feed and are fed by their hierarchical religious language. Social change, it seems, is possible given transformations in the frameworks that make up any cultural system. While North Owl's journey from living with the Kesh and inside the nonhuman community to living with the Condor and outside this community, ultimately to return to the Kesh, represents a journey between opposite ends of a gendered spectrum, *Always Coming Home* does not frame this spectrum as natural and something to be dealt with using separatist strategies. As a result, Le Guin's book contributes much to ecofeminist theorizing, embracing much in cultural ecofeminist thought but positing additional, more complex theoretical questions.

A DOOR INTO OCEAN

If we evaluate *The Wanderground*, *Always Coming Home*, and Slonczewski's *A Door Into Ocean* using a strict cultural ecofeminist rubric, then their authors' creations of separate spaces for the ideological positions they critique and celebrate display quite adequately the gender associations upon which cultural ecofeminism bases its thinking. *The Wanderground*'s potently masculine, aggressively sexual and technological City invades an ecofeminist wilderness of liberated and highly evolved women. *Always Coming Home*'s reestablished City of Man, which like its ancestral Industrial Age lives "outside the world," intrudes upon a revived ecocentric culture and this culture's Earth-based spirituality. *A Door Into Ocean*'s colonialist and patriarchal planet Valedon threatens the sovereign, all-female, all-waterworld Shora, whose inhabitants have a remarkable knowledge of ecology and a strong sense of place. Slonczewski's clear gendering of colonialist politics and ecological wisdom as male and female, respectively, operates in much the same way as Gearhart's and Le Guin's gendering of similar ideological stances—as cultural ecofeminist polemic. But like *Always Coming Home*'s ecofeminism, *A Door Into Ocean*'s goes beyond this polemic to fashion more complex understandings of gender and thus more effective liberatory strategies for women and nonhuman nature.

A shift toward a more critical position characterizes Slonczewski's ecofeminism, but as with *Always Coming Home* this shift does not involve a wholesale dismissal of cultural ecofeminist ideas. Read together, Le Guin's and Slonczewski's books provide a full sense of what I believe is the ecofeminist position they both ultimately participate in and argue for, a position that is aligned with the ecofeminist Ynestra King's resistance to an academic fragmentation of the movement into dichotomous theoretical brands. I will explicate *A Door Into Ocean* within this context shortly, after taking a moment to note that King's *dialectical* ecofeminism—a label I am adopting from Catriona Sandilands (1999)—at once rejects essentialist gender associations and revalues nurturance, interdependence, and other subordinate yet more ecologically conscious precepts.[6] What sets this ecofeminism apart from the cultural ecofeminism of Plant, Collard, and Gearhart is its anti-essentialist stance; what sets it apart from the rationalist feminism of Prentice and Biehl is its open-mindedness to alternative forms of critical engagement, such as spirituality, intuition, passivity, and emotion.

King (1989) argues that ecofeminism must be revised to embrace the more complex social conscience of rationalist positions while still preserving the ecological conscience of cultural ecofeminism. She admits that in choosing nature over culture and feminine values over masculine values, cultural ecofeminism does not adequately question these illusory dualisms. Demonstrating a more constructionist standpoint, she writes, "Women's ecological sensitivity and life orientation is a socialized perspective that could be social-ized right out of [them] depending on [their] day-to-day lives" (King 1989: 23). Continuing, she notes, "There is no reason to believe that women placed in positions of patriarchal power will act any differently from men" (King 1989: 23). Women's ecological sensitivity is context specific, not universal. Just as women can be healers, nurturers, or defenders of nonhuman nature, given different cultural contexts they might also oppose these traits. Like-wise, whereas men can be culturally programmed to be militaristic, other contexts might determine them to be caring.

Such critical positions on gender and gendered value categories help free ecofeminism from some potentially devastating theoretical and practical lim-itations, the same limitations that hinder *The Wanderground* from today pro-viding a more effective and applicable critique. In King's ecofeminism the transformative impulse is not tied to the idea that change can happen only within a supposedly universal feminine social or spiritual framework, and in the absence of an equally universal masculinity. Instead, ecofeminist reform begins in comprehending gender assumptions as constructed social phenom-ena. King's (1989: 23) final image of a more effective ecofeminism is one that welcomes a multiplicity of views not strictly constructionist or rational-ist: "Ecofeminism suggests . . . a recognition that although the nature-culture dualism is a product of culture, we can nonetheless *consciously choose* not to sever the woman-nature connection by joining male culture. Rather, we can use it as a vantage point for creating a different kind of culture and politics that would integrate intuitive, spiritual, and rational forms of knowledge, embracing both science and magic insofar as they enable us to transform the nature-culture distinction and to envision and create a free, ecological soci-ety." King blends cultural ecofeminism and rationalist feminism in a way that creates a new category for the movement, a category deeply concerned with removing the extremes of these two positions while embracing what is most valuable in each. Such an ecofeminism understands woman-nature con-nections, man/nature disconnections, and nature/culture dualisms as malle-able cultural products that must be evaluated using a range of critical voices and tools—from the engaged democratic processes of rationalist feminism to the deeply personal, ecospiritual reflections of cultural ecofeminism.

As with Gearhart's and Le Guin's speculative fictions, Slonczewski's novel shares with cultural ecofeminism the dual goals of censuring patriar-chy's social and ecological oppressions as well as highlighting the ecological conscience associated with women. And like Le Guin's book, Slonczewski's develops its ecofeminist position further by adding a level of complexity characteristic of the dialectical ecofeminism just reviewed. Shora's inhabi-tants, Sharers, are much like the women of *The Wanderground* and the Vil-lage dwellers of *Always Coming Home* in that they have traits demonstrating their deep connection to place. Physically, the "breathmicrobes" of the Shoran atmosphere turn Sharers' skin deep purple, a preventable phenomenon they accept as part of dwelling on Shora. Their lungs have evolved to allow long stints of breathlessness under water. Conceptually, the notion of sharing that gives Shora's inhabitants their name erases the hierarchies of dualistic, patriarchal thinking; their expressions "learnsharing, worksharing, [and] lovesharing" nullify any paradigm denying that "each force has an equal and opposite force" (Slonczewski 1986: 36). And intellectually Sharers under-stand their lives as dependent on an intact ecological web. When asked why she does not spray the living rafts, upon which Sharers make their homes, with a pesticide when parasites threaten them, Merwen—a native of Shora—responds, "Then seasilk would choke the raft. And fingershells would go hungry, and tubeworms die of the poison; then fish and octopus would have nothing, and what would Sharers eat?" (Slonczewski 1986: 60). Their physi-cal, conceptual, and intellectual embeddedness in ecological place sets the Sharers apart from their patriarchal oppressors, whose intrusion into Shora constitutes much of the plot of Slonczewski's novel.

Valedon's people, Valans, know the Sharers as "women-like creatures who lived in the endless sea, women whose men were never seen, who subsisted on seaworms and could dive deep beyond light's reach without going mad" (Slonczewski 1986: 9). This perspective shrouds the Sharers in a mystery of otherness that for the Valans justifies attempts at their exploita-tion by a patriarchy cemented to hierarchical value structures. Historically Valedon had a native population, known derogatorily as "Trolls," that "passed away when the godlike Primes"—who were modern humans, but are now extinct due to nuclear catastrophe—"came to remodel the planet . . . to human standards" (Slonczewski 1986: 36). As "creatures," Sharers, too, are threatened by a new manifestation of power; the rulers of the universal politi-cal system of which Valedon is a part—the Patriarchy—want to open up Shora for mineral exploration and textile markets. Sharer compliance is nec-essary for this to happen, but since increased economic exploitation threatens the lifeforms of Shora, such compliance will not happen. Valan trade there has already brought on much ocean noise, drowning out the communications of animals essential to Shoran ecological integrity. The traders' applications of poisons to the Shoran sea has also threatened life. Thus the Sharers defend their planet against these, and many more, intrusions.

The Patriarchy was formed to regulate independent governments away from the dangerous uses of military power that ended the reign of the Primes. But the events of *A Door Into Ocean* suggest little distinction between the violent use of nuclear weaponry by the Primes and the violent use of eco-nomic weaponry by those now in the Patriarchy. The Patriarchy claims to follow "the lesson of the dead gods: too many people smashed too many atoms—and planets, in the end," but its support of Valedon's social, politi-cal, and economic exploitation of Shora demonstrates that it fails to see this exploitation as another way of smashing planets (Slonczewski 1986: 21). In the same way that Le Guin extrapolates the Condor from the poisoned society of the Industrial Age, Slonczewski relates the Patriarchy to the extinct Primes to urge a radical move away from the logic of domination and its consequential social, political, and ecological abuses. This concern about patriarchy is not specific to cultural ecofeminism. As a feminist mode, ecofeminism is always critical of patriarchy's logic of domination. But explicit in *A Door Into Ocean* is the cultural ecofeminist view of "feminine" ways of knowing and being as promising the opposition needed to move toward a more ecologically conscious society and politics. In this way the cultural ecofeminist moments of Slonczewski's book share much with their equivalent moments in Gearhart's book.

The stark contrast between Valedon's social and political norms and the life ways of the Sharers leads to gendered ideological collisions as Valans attempt to take possession of Shora. While the outcomes of these collisions seemingly favor masculine power, in the end the Sharers overthrow their colonial oppressors by using what Slonczewski's book overtly considers a feminine will. Most tellingly indicating the radical cultural ecofeminism of this novel, the Sharers live in a female separatist ecotopia where the absence of men permits certain values to thrive: respecting social and ecological interconnectedness, affirming and nurturing life, and building communicative networks. Sharer science is a science of life, their intellectual supremacy in biology used not to destroy but to nurture ecological systems. Their politics is one of open communication between all of Shora's raft communities during events called Gatherings. And Sharers are pacifists. In an instance that reveals the intertwining of their scientific knowledge and valuing of life, their political methodologies, and their pacifism, at one Gathering a Sharer named Yinerva proposes to use biological warfare to rid Shora of "the Valan pestilence" that threatens "Not only Sharer children and survival . . . , but all the other creatures of Shora, the lesser sisters, seaswallowers, fanwings, rafts—from snail to swallower" (Slonczewski 1986: 309). The group, however, ultimately chooses to preserve their nonviolent ways and instead to conquer the Valans with what the defeated Valan general calls "bloodless 'invasions'" (Slonczewski 1986: 395). The Sharers' nonviolent techniques for resisting Valan aggression include whitetrance—a form of "Gandhian discipline" in which a Sharer grows pale, still, and unresponsive to outside threats—as well as boycotting Valan goods (Slonczewski 2001: par. 31).

Read as a cultural ecofeminist text, *A Door Into Ocean* demonstrates the potential for "feminine" values to triumph over "masculine" impositions. But because the reason for Shora's ultimate defeat of Valedon and the Patriarchy is only partially tied to gendered values, it would be an incomplete judgment to deem Slonczewski's novel a work of hard cultural ecofeminism without considering the range of its critical thinking. For one, Valedon's racism also instigates its military's retreat. While Valan patriarchy indeed cannot beat down Shoran ways of life, Valan racism cannot permit Valedon's army to succeed in its colonialist task. One of the most effective ways the Sharers defeat the Valans is not by conscious tactic but by possessing a racial characteristic that signifies for the Valans various substandard associations: purple skin. From the perspective of the Valan mindset, Sharers are low creatures. They are natives who "don't think like civilized people," who are "just naked women," and who do not "acknowledge the authority of Valedon" (Slonczewski 1986: 275, 253, 249). When the skin of the Valan occupiers begins to take on the marker of Sharer nativeness, they fear the "Purple Plague" (Slonczewski 1986: 299). Troop morale plummets, contributing to the ultimate withdrawal of the army.

While this particular criticism of racism is perhaps and at first odd in its suggestion, against history, that colonialist fears of the predefined Other can protect colonized cultures—rather than justify and prompt militaristic and/or economic endeavor against them—it is nonetheless crucial in its recognition that colonial power is a conglomeration of several oppressive forces, including racism and patriarchy. Thus, *A Door Into Ocean* shares the theoretical positions of Prentice, Biehl, and King, who also do not limit their critiques of oppression to patriarchy alone. Prentice's and Biehl's rationalist feminisms, and King's dialectical ecofeminism, complement Murray Bookchin's social ecology, which targets *hierarchy* as the foundation upon which sexism, racism, and other modes of domination are built (hence his attacks on deep ecology, a movement that wants to reorder the anthropocentric/ecocentric hierarchy). According to social ecology, interrogating any one of these forms of oppression alone does not achieve the complete critical assessment and revision that interrogating their underlying motivating force can. As Mellor (1997: 158) observes, "Patriarchy only exists as one form of hierarchy, it is neither the original, nor the primary oppression." Gaard (1998: 43) also makes this point when defining *social* ecofeminism: "Features unique to social ecofeminism include . . . its analysis of the hierarchical structure of oppression as even more descriptive than the specific forms of oppression." *A Door Into Ocean* moves into such a critical territory, beyond the limited range of cultural ecofeminism's exclusive focus on patriarchy—and often its support of alternative valuations that are hierarchical nonetheless—and into a focus on questioning together patriarchy, racial essentialism, and anthropocentrism. Such a complete critical evaluation is necessary for the total dissolution of hierarchy, in general, that would liberate nonhuman nature from human tyranny as it also liberates oppressed humans from oppressive ones.

Though *A Door Into Ocean*'s focus on race, or hierarchy more generally, is secondary to its primary focus on gender and patriarchy, the novel still moves strongly away from strict cultural ecofeminism. Operating on patriarchy not simply to reverse its assumptions, but more so to include it in a broader critical analysis of gender assumptions in general, Slonczewski's book tests cultural ecofeminism and patriarchal essentialism alike with two of its characters, the male Spinel and the female Jade. As Susan Stratton (2001: par. 22) notes, "Gender duality [in *A Door Into Ocean*] is challenged both by the successful adaptation of a Valedonian male teenager to Sharer ways and by the fact that the most vicious of Valedonian soldiers is female." These characterizations complicate essentialist notions and open the door for ecofeminism to look more at the social than the so-called innate origins of male and female behavior and relationships with nonhuman nature.

Slonczewski's novel is in part a bildungsroman about Spinel, an adolescent boy from Valedon who goes to Shora, experiences life there, and ultimately chooses to stay. Spinel's acceptance of Sharer ways, however, comes after his interior battle with himself over the patriarchal ideology he has come to know. Going through hard times financially, Spinel's parents arrange for him to seek opportunity on Shora. The Sharers promote the move, for Spinel presents them with the opportunity to study masculinity and to prove that a man can become a Sharer. But Spinel is not so excited. It is outrageous to him that there are not any men on Shora, and he believes that "A world without fathers could have no place for him" (Slonczewski 1986: 22). Coming from a hierarchical society Spinel sees the equality among Sharers as the product of "bizarre logic"; to him the planet is "ridiculous" (Slonczewski 1986: 61). And as Spinel's exposure to the Shoran atmosphere turns him purple, he demands a medicine that will curtail the phenomenon.

With his compulsory defense of the heterosexual family unit, his hierarchical logic, and his unwillingness to experience difference, Spinel embodies essentialist notions of masculinity. But Spinel is not the subject of essentialist contention. Central to Slonczewski's argument is that masculinity is a socialized characteristic, and this is made obvious as Spinel embeds himself more and more into Shoran life, shedding his socialized masculinity and adopting a social and ecological conscience. Interestingly, this embedding begins after he witnesses the wonders of Shoran ecology: "Now he had time to absorb the silent drama that pulsed below the waves. Hungry eels hid in wait beneath raft seedlings, which now dotted the sea like copper medals. A fanwing's egg stretched and strained until a tadpole burst out and flittered away, to swim and grow until it sprouted wings. At the coral forest, a beakfish crunched the hard stalks with enormous jaws that never tired. After some minutes of this calciferous grazing, a puff of sand would spout from its tail. Spinel wondered how long a beach a beakfish could fill, were the sand not destined to fall several kilometers below. Spinel was now more than simply curious about Shora. Something compelled him to come to grips with this place that was inexorably becoming a part of him" (Slonczewski 1986: 100). Afterwards, "Spinel was now more than simply curious about Shora. Something compelled him to come to grips with this place that was inexorably becoming a part of him" (Slonczewski 1986: 100). That "Something" is likely the very nonhuman nature within which he overtly experiences his embeddedness as his skin deepens to purple and his ocean dives increase in depth and duration. Spinel's newfound sense of place ultimately leads him to join the Sharers in defending their planet against Valan exploitation, his sea change expressed in the final words of the novel as he swims away from the spacecraft that would have taken him back to Valedon: "a friendly fanwing dipped and soared overhead like a hand beckoning, Come, lovesharer, come home" (Slonczewski 1986: 403).

That a male can become a "lovesharer" is one part of the constructionist ecofeminist claim of *A Door Into Ocean*. The other is that given the cultural atmosphere a woman can embody the worst of masculine aggressiveness. As Chief of Staff of the Valan army, Jade is a woman whose militarism challenges essentialist notions of femininity and the idea that violence and hostility are sex specific. About militaristic conditioning, ecofeminist scholar Janis Birkeland (1993: 35) writes, "Men are taught to despise and distance themselves from their 'feminine' side, or their emotions and feeling." Slonczewski's narrative shows that such conditioning is inscribable on both men and women. Jade derogatorily nicknames the Sharers "catfish," placing them at the bottom of an ontological hierarchy that denies species equality and justifies Valan oppressions against Shoran natives. "Catfish aren't human," Jade says, "they're Vermin, and that's how to treat them" (Slonczewski 1986: 323). Jade admits that it is her duty to kill, as she also administers a range of tortures in an attempt to crack the Sharer's nonviolent protests. In Slonczewski's world masculinity is a socialized trait; militarism and violent aggression do not emerge simply from being male but are characteristics etched on any sex by genderless, oppressive institutions.

CONCLUSION

Stephanie Lahar (1993: 97) asks, "Is there a way to know whether there were ever times and places when human beings lived in easy cooperation with each other and the nonhuman environment, without the sexist, oppressive, and exploitive complex of power relations we call patriarchy? Is seeking such times and places useful in empowering women today, by portraying model societies in which women either shared or held primary power?" As works of science fiction, Gearhart's, Le Guin's, and Slonczewski's novels all imagine such times and places. But their positions, like ecofeminism itself, are diverse. Espousing the multiplicity of perspectives within ecofeminism, Lee Quinby (1990: 123) notices that ecofeminism "has combated ecological destruction and patriarchal domination without succumbing to the totalizing impulses of masculinist politics," embracing as political strategy a plurality of theoretical positions rather than a single, hegemonic stance. The ecofeminist texts reviewed in this chapter confirm Quinby's point, at least regarding science fiction's ecofeminist theorizations.

Often challenged as essentialist in its judgments, *The Wanderground* embraces as political strategy the spatial separation of men and women as well as the safeguarding and uninhibited self-realization of both women and nonhuman nature associated with this separation. Ecotopian? Perhaps. But ecotopian visions have transformative potential, if not to lay a literal groundwork then certainly to posit an intellectual compass for moving toward a new ground. And in Gearhart's novel, that compass is one necessitated by the experiences of women and nonhuman nature during the time of the book's composition—the 1970s—when both feminists and environmentalists were pushing the boundaries of dominant ideology and reaching for new and effective critical methodologies.

Always Coming Home and *A Door Into Ocean* also embrace cultural ecofeminism, positing as a critical strategy the intellectual consideration of gender difference. But these books intrinsically question their own considerations. Le Guin's work does not locate gendered difference in inflexible biological determinations, instead highlighting the malleability of the structures and symbolisms determining female and male relationships with nonhuman nature, and with each other. Slonczewski's book expands the ecofeminist critique of patriarchy to a broader social critique of hierarchy as it also underscores gendered behavior as specific to the atmospheres constructing such behavior, regardless of sex. By doing so, *Always Coming Home* and *A Door Into Ocean* develop on cultural ecofeminism without watering down what is most important in its message: the liberation of women and nonhuman nature from oppression. These liberations demand theoretical and practical diversity. *The Wanderground*, *Always Coming Home*, and *A Door Into Ocean* together offer us literary explorations of this diversity. These books, emerging as they do at the moment of ecofeminism's maturity, illustrate science fiction's deep interest in social and ecological liberation.

NOTES

1. This chapter also appears in Eric C. Otto's (2012) *Green Speculations: Science Fiction and Transformative Environmentalism* and is published here with permission of The Ohio State University Press.

2. The poststructuralist theorists who inform Armbruster's discussion are Teresa de Lauretis and Donna Haraway, who both declare identity as the always-shifting product of "multiple axes of difference," rather than as the static product of nature or other singular or ranked factors (Armbruster 1998: 105).

3. On the connections between cultural ecofeminism and deep ecology, Mary Mellor (1997: 208) writes, "Cultural ecofeminists and deep ecologists share a strategy of reversing valuations in the classic culture (man)/nature (woman) dualism: deep ecologists urge humans to

subordinate themselves to nature (biocentrism), and cultural ecofeminists celebrate women's connections to nature and many traditionally feminine characteristics."

4. Even Prentice (1988: 9) admits that (cultural) ecofeminism "reminds all people of the fragile, endangered, and inextricable inter-dependence of all life—including human life—and the planet."

5. With respect to the critical possibilities of cultural ecofeminist essentialism, Alaimo (2000: 8) also warns against rationalist feminism's "hasty dismissal" of ecofeminist arguments that are labeled "essentialist." She references Noël Sturgeon (1997: 11), who writes, "Essentialist moments in ecofeminism, given particular historical conditions, are part of creating a shifting and strategic identification of the relation between 'women' and 'nature' that has political purposes."

6. On King's dialectical ecofeminism, Sandilands (1999: 18) notes, "King's project was to transcend the 'either/or' assumptions inherent in the debate between rationalist-materialist humanism and metaphysical-feminist naturalism, to create a dialectical feminism that incorporates the best insights of both traditions."

Chapter Two

Barbara Kingsolver's *Animal Dreams*

Ecofeminist Subversion of Western Myth

Theda Wrede

Barbara Kingsolver, in *Animal Dreams* (1990a), revisits Western myth to examine its constructions of the land, women, and cultural minorities.[1] As a discourse of the dominant culture, this male myth, she feels, merits rethinking.[2] Though it survives the scrutiny of her ecofeminist politics, Western myth emerges as something quite different in her work. Calling into question such traditional values as self-reliance and domination over a wildly "virginal" utopia or "non-place," Kingsolver's ecofeminist narrative affirms love and respect for an actual, rural Southwestern landscape. The novel thus intuits how ecocriticism and feminism agree in a deep structural sense by opening themselves up to relational connections between humans and the land.

While critics have pointed out the novel's usage of myth in affirming an ecofeminist message, they leave unexplained what precisely enables the attitudes of care and respect for the "Other" that characterize both environmentalist and feminist premises. This chapter will fill this gap in Kingsolver criticism by drawing on Karen Warren's, Val Plumwood's, and Annette Kolodny's constructivist ecofeminisms in conjunction with Jessica Benjamin's psychoanalytic theories to discern the psychological assumptions that underlie Kingsolver's ecofeminist message. I argue that Kingsolver's ecofeminist rewriting of Western myth is based on the discovery of an authentic, pre-socialization, psychic state of intersubjectivity that traditional (male) myth can only suggest but not provide. In her new myth, this authenticity enables her heroine to "create" a home, rather than venture out to "find" a utopian place, by caring for and respecting the real space. In opening the possibility for environmentally sensitive interactions with landscape, Kingsolver's constructivist ecofeminist politics do not rule out men's potential for developing relational connections with nature. Yet she distinguishes a central impediment to male relationality in a cultural script that, expecting men to be independent, often thwarts their intersubjectivity. Conversely, emphasizing relationships, women's social role facilitates relationality.[3]

Applying a variety of approaches that range from a poststructuralist reading of fictional spaces to investigations of the narrative's subversive return to myth (especially vis-à-vis gynocentric emotion),[4] a number of critics have focused on Kingsolver's attempts to offer readers an edifying environmentalist—and ecofeminist—lesson. "In *Animal Dreams*," Naomi Jacobs argues, "familiar themes and tropes from a popular genre [the Western] provide the sugarcoating for a radical challenge to American ideologies of macho individualism and justifiable aggression (2003: 9).[5] And Connie Sue Watts points out the novel's ecofeminist didacticism: "By exposing some of our national myths, Barbara Kingsolver, like other ecofeminists, is attempting to redefine and transform our social consciousness. Kingsolver's main political and social concerns in this novel echo ecofeminist ideology and its advocacy of a transformation of consciousness that acknowledges and respects the environment" (1994: 53). Similarly, Patti Capel Swartz explains, "Kingsolver's writing is 'women's writing' that does resonate with possibilities. Although [Silko] discusses important issues, these issues are not presented 'objectively,' i.e. unemotionally. Politics, the environment, and spirituality are rather approached through personal experience and intra- and inter-personal connections" (1993: 66).[6]

Other critics, nevertheless, contest the novel's environmentalist stance, particularly by sounding out its proclaimed liberalism. Maureen Ryan labels the novel "lite" fiction and condemns its "aggressively political correct[ness]" that makes it "good for us" like a "healthy" dish (1995: 77, 81). Krista Comer takes issue particularly with what she perceives as a conservative use of Western myth. She contends that through "an antimodern and antitechnology bent, redemptive landscapes, Indian mysticism, wide-open spaces, and utopic possibility," Kingsolver actually reinforces tropes of Western masculinity in her fictional wilderness landscape (Comer 1999: 219-220). The novel describes, Comer states, a "flight from history" that relishes the primitive—and male—ideal on its search for an "idealized Southwest" (1999: 230). Kingsolver's use of Western myth is, indeed, ambiguous at first glance, and her often upfront didacticism risks harming her environmental message. However, I suggest, the author merges the traditional trope with her green politics so that her environmentalist stance *thrives* on a nostalgic return to Western myth. Specifically, Kingsolver judiciously engages in a dialogue with dominant discursive paradigms not only to assert the losses that attend the spreading of modern capitalist society but also, and more importantly, to overcome these nostalgic tendencies and envision alternative figurations.

THEORETICAL FRAMEWORK: ECOFEMINISM AND PSYCHOANALYSIS

Karen Warren's (2000) and Val Plumwood's (1991 and 1997) philosophies provide a useful theoretical framework to scrutinize Kingsolver's ecofeminist message, whereas Annette Kolodny's studies (1975a and 1984) help the reader perceive Kingsolver's careful appropriation and subversion of the myth in relation to its historical and literary contexts. Noting the significance of language in expressing attitudes and behavior, these theorists also understand language as a source of social transformation. They unveil the discursive constructedness of cultural dualities (opposing humans and nature) and gender hierarchies (placing men above women) and offer a solution in a "feminine" language that conveys a "feminine" relationship to the surrounding world, one that is generally characterized by "reciprocity." To Warren particularly, women's narrative accounts can reveal feminine values (embodied in their intimate connection with the land and other cultures) and contribute to both ecological betterment and female empowerment.[7] Warren observes, "Because the dismantling of patriarchal conceptual frameworks is a feminist issue, *how* one climbs a mountain and *how* one narrates—or tells a story—about the experience of climbing also are *feminist issues.* In this way, ecofeminism makes visible why, at a conceptual level, environmental ethics is a feminist issue" (Warren 2000: 29). She uses such expressions as a "loving perception" and a "loving eye"—"one that constantly 'must look and listen and check and question,'"—to characterize the desired relational connection with nature (Warren 2000: 28). Like Warren, Plumwood focuses on the dual oppression of women and nature and emphasizes the power of language to affect changes. Based on the shared experience, women, Plumwood asserts, must speak up for nature because nature cannot speak for itself or at least is generally not "heard" when it does: "Our speech for the other is made possible by the commonality of the centric structure, for as ecofeminists we speak as those who are ourselves oppressed in a different area, as women, and we are able to transfer our understanding to the other's oppression" (Plumwood 1997: 350). Women, she proposes, rather than speak in place of nature, will act as its "interpreters" (Plumwood 1997: 351). To Plumwood, this connection between nature and women must necessarily entail women's active involvement in environmental protection.

It comes as no surprise, then, that both Warren and Plumwood emphasize the need for cultural encounters, a "*collage* or *mosaic*, a *tapestry* of voices springing from the plurality of female 'felt experiences'" (Warren 2000: 30). They assert an "inclusive" "feminist ethic" that voices the experiences of all oppressed persons and does not claim to be objective" (Warren 2000: 31). Significantly, the theorists argue that by positioning themselves within this variety of voices and experiences, women more readily discover a sense of the female self—as part of a diverse environment with which they are neither identical nor inimical. A "collage" opposes "the inferiorization of both women and nature," Plumwood says, that "is grounded in rationalism, and the connections of both to the inferiorizing of the body, hierarchical concepts of labor, and disembedded and individualist accounts of self" (1991: 173). If (masculine) rationalism, associated with an androcentric worldview that opposes relationality, is at the origin of social inequalities, a solution springs from a relational self that is open to all that seems "other."

In her analyses of "mythic" landscapes, Kolodny, unlike Plumwood and Warren, focuses on the realm of literature, art, and history—a focus that is especially valuable in elucidating the interdependencies of myth and nostalgia in Kingsolver's novel. In her first book, *The Lay of the Land* (1975a), Kolodny presents male settlers' destructive interaction with the land as a consequence of those discursive structures that are sustained by the ambivalent and nostalgic desires either to return to a "nurturing," "female" landscape or to possess a presumably "virginal" wilderness.[8] Discussing the frontier painter John James Audubon, the writers Philip Freneau and James Fenimore Cooper, and the politician/philosopher Thomas Jefferson, she uncovers in their language and art a coalescence of loss and guilt, for their entrance into the wild meant penetration and thus the violation of the pristine landscape of their desire. Metaphors that feminize the land, Kolodny explains, have an immense attraction for settlers in that such tropes suggest the possibility of recovery of the pre-oedipal imagined merger/omnipotence relinquished with socialization's emphasis on separation. At the same time, they allow the land to be treated like "the female," to be subject to "conquest and mastery" (1975a: 133).[9]

Conversely, scrutinizing women's writing about the frontier experience in her second book *The Land Before Her: Fantasy and Experience of the American Frontiers, 1630-1860* (1984), Kolodny notes that a "female discourse" about the wilderness exposes an "alternative metaphorical design" (1984: xii). Women, "having . . . long been barred from the fantasy garden"—a consequence of the male myth—"quite literally set about planting gardens in these wilderness places" (1984: xiii). Women's gardens manifest the potential of relational connections with the land that are based on appreciation, care, and respect:

> "Paradise" implied radically different places when used by men and by women. For men the term (with all its concomitant psycho-sexual associations) echoed an invitation for mastery and possession of the vast new continent. For women, by contrast, it denoted domesticity. Thus, while men sought new Edens and created new Arcadias for themselves, working "the keen adze" and altering the landscape to make it comply with their dreams of receptive and bountiful realms, women patched Pine Tree quilts, appliquéd counterpanes

with brightly colored Rose of Sharon designs, and cultivated small gardens in order "to render Home a Paradise." (1984: 54)

Women's "fantasies" of a domestic Eden (as opposed to men's fantasies of a female wilderness) permitted them to escape male domination and envision the new land as a "potential sanctuary for an idealized domesticity" (Kolodny 1984: xiii). Yet whereas in *The Lay of the Land* Kolodny explains the psychology behind the mythic male dream, in *The Land Before Her* she leaves women's reactions to the frontier unexplained. A first task for the critic, then, will be a consideration of the psychological basis of women's attitude of nonviolence and respect for a more domestic wilderness.

Jessica Benjamin's model of intersubjectivity in *The Bonds of Love* (1988) serves well to back and explain, from a psychoanalytic perspective, constructivist ecofeminist paradigms that stress interrelationships and refute domination/subordination models.[10] Her theories enrich Kolodny's discussion with a vision of human interaction beyond dominant cultural parameters.[11] In her fundamental revision of the Freudian model, Benjamin draws on object relations theory. Where Freudian models stipulate that maturity and autonomy can only spring, during the oedipal phase of childhood development, from a radical separation from the mother (the first "object") and a shift of alliance toward the father, Benjamin proposes a pre-oedipal (preceding socialization) potential for interrelationships. Thus, taking into account both girls' and boys' gradual differentiation and acquisition of autonomy, Benjamin argues that autonomy need not depend wholly on separation and domination—it can be fostered through "mutual recognition," a concept that is based on D. W. Winnicott's (1971) transitional object but includes the mother's own need for selfhood. Mutual recognition necessitates the interplay of difference, of giving and taking, asserting and denying. In mutuality, we recognize a process of individuation that rests in the awareness of both our dependency on others and their dependence on us. Benjamin states, "The combination of resonance and difference that the mother offers can open the way to a recognition that transcends mastery and mechanical response, to a recognition that is based on *mutuality*" (1988: 35). All the same, Benjamin is aware of how culturally constructed notions of gender determine either control or submission. Even as she agrees with the constructivist critique of gender, she shows that power is only part of the story of social domination.[12] She contributes to the feminist dialogue with an investigation of the psychic structures that make domination and subordination possible and thus pave the way for social and cultural hierarchies.

Benjamin shows that mutual recognition is actually a result of a great effort, in which finding the authentic potential for intersubjectivity is predicated on the parents' understanding of the infant's complex needs. Drawing on Hegel's master-slave dialectic, she notes that an infant's growing awareness of differentiation and agency is contingent on the outcomes of games of control it plays with the other (often the mother). These "games" become dangerous when the infant "controls" the mother, Benjamin argues, and she, in turn, "ceas[ing] to exist" as a separate unity, cannot grant the toddler the recognition it needs to gain a sense of agency. The toddler thus experiences "emptiness and loss of connection that result from his fearful power" (1988: 35).[13] But domination or subordination often follows along gender lines. Benjamin states, "Separation-individuation . . . becomes a gender issue, and recognition and independence are . . . organized within the frame of gender" (qtd. in Steele 1997: 88). If a cultural script demands a boy's absolute independence, girls are often expected to maintain relationships and even relinquish their individual selfhood. While boys may thus suffer from the feelings of separateness and emptiness, girls experience the loss of self through something like a "merger" with others, one that negates her autonomy.

A recurring pattern of domination or submission inhibits the development of viable relationships with others, whereas recognition enables intersubjectivity: "The decisive problem remains *recognizing the other.* Establishing *my*self . . . means winning the recognition of the other, and this, in turn, means I must finally acknowledge the other as existing for *him*self and not just for me" (Benjamin 1988: 36). Benjamin claims that an emotional exchange—"the affective content of the mother-child exchange"—and attunement to the other are expressions of mutuality and a more general "blurring of boundaries" with the external world (1988: 31). These make possible respect, empathy, and recognition of the other as an agent. Only then can the self also experience the desired recognition by the other. Mutual recognition or "intersubjectivity," then, describes a "paradoxical mixture of otherness and togetherness" (Benjamin 1988: 14–15).

Benjamin and Kolodny, along with Warren and Plumwood, believe in the possibility of change; they envision alternatives to social value binaries in attitudes of care, mutual recognition, and what Kolodny calls "reciprocity and communality" (1975a: 145). None of the theorists suggests that men and women are biologically predisposed to their social roles.[14] But they agree that a significant change can only occur when our cultural values shift from individualism to community, from radical separation to relationality.

If the relational model could potentially figure as a solution to the problem of primary loss, the pain of separation, and the consequent difficulty of domination and submission, the question arises in how far the model could also set an example for human interactions with Southwestern landscape. In their emphases on values of care, emotional attunement, and mutual recognition, all four theorists offer an effective theoretical foundation for my discussion of Kingsolver's relational account in *Animal Dreams.* Through "mutual recognition" and "reciprocity" Codi Nolina, by the end of the novel, overcomes her feelings of loss and estrangement. Kingsolver thus explores a female double allegiance to the land and the community that enables her heroine to create a home in the wilderness. That this allegiance is reciprocal is evident in the heroine's emerging emotional attachment to a culturally diverse community and in her grassroots environmental activism which correlate with both the community's and the land's ability to provide a psychological and physical refuge.

BARBARA KINGSOLVER'S *ANIMAL DREAMS*

Codi enters her mythic quest for authenticity with expectations spurred by a loss of meaningful human connections that affects her conception of self. Kingsolver's heroine returns to her hometown of Grace, the rural enclave in New Mexico she had left fourteen years prior. She hopes that recovering her personal past may restore her sense of identity: "I believe I was hoping that . . . I would step off the bus and land smack in the middle of a sense of belonging. . . . home at last" (Kingsolver 1990a: 12). Kingsolver identifies this "home" mainly through its rural community whose entanglements with the contemporary world *and* the past Codi must comprehend in order to find—or make—a home. Her search, therefore, does not end with arrival. It begins.

Central to Codi's experiences are her encounters with nature. Stepping off the bus in Grace, Codi assumes a knowing tone that implies familiarity with the place and its picturesque view despite her long absence: "Grace is made of things that erode too slowly to be noticed: red granite canyon walls, orchards of sturdy old fruit trees past their prime, a shamelessly unpolluted sky. The houses were built in no big hurry back when labor was taken for granted, and now were in no big hurry to decay. Arthritic mesquite trees grew out of impossible crevices in the cliffs, looking as if they could adapt to life on Mars if need be" (1990a: 8). With sky, orchards, and canyon in the background, the town and its houses in the foreground, the scene strikes the eye as a painterly flush of color and textures. The subject matter of the "painting" is clearly the pastoral life of pre-industrialized agricultural society, complete with an "unpolluted" sky and a suggestion of life unfolding at a deliberate pace—"the houses were built in no big hurry." The pervasive images of age and death ("erode," "past their prime," "decay," "arthritic") contribute to, rather than deflate, the scene's picturesque qualities. Loss, after all, always galvanizes the pastoral dream. However, colored by nostalgic memories and desires to relive the past, Codi's perceptions of this landscape also indicate, incongruously, that the past is very much a part of the present:[15] Although "past their prime," the fruit trees and the "arthritic mesquite trees" survive in an inhospitable environment—the "impossible crevices in the cliffs"—and thus provide testimony not only to an otherwise forgotten past but also to the power of endurance.

It is precisely that persistence of the past in Grace, in the face of all odds, that carries hope. Because the "unpolluted sky" reveals a connection with those past times in which all skies were still clean, it suggests a certain strength and tenaciousness that Codi describes as "shameless." Therefore, "Grace would turn out," she observes, "to be the yardstick I'd been using to measure all other places, like the mysterious worn-out photo that storybook orphans carry from place to place, never realizing till the end that it's really their home" (Kingsolver 1990a: 12).

However, Codi's view of Grace's small downtown as a deathscape offers a stark contrast with this scene of rural felicity. Codi experiences a new form of estrangement that is mirrored in descriptions of the town's main street: "There wasn't a soul on the street today and I thought of those movies in which a town is wiped clean of its inhabitants, for one reason or another—a nuclear holocaust, say, or a deadly mutant virus—leaving only a shell of consumer goods. The point, I think, is to make some statement about how we get carried away with all our trappings" (Kingsolver 1990a: 11). Phrases like "nuclear holocaust" and "deadly mutant virus" indicate the suddenness of death that leaves an eerie shell of life—"of consumer goods"—behind. But what stays behind and what sudden death whisks away together announce a neat division between the essential in life and the inessential that all too often "carries" us "away with all our trappings": the "leering" shop windows of Grace contain a "ferocious display of polyester," and overdressed "headless mannequins" signify the lack of essence (encoded in the missing head) of blatantly displaced objects. Juxtaposing this dreadful sight with her own reflection in one of the windows—in "Levi's and Billy Idol haircut"—Codi implies that, though more fashionable, she feels as alienated and shell-like as these decorations (Kingsolver 1990a: 11).

Further compromising an earlier pastoral moment and aggravating Codi's ambivalence toward her hometown is the sight of the copper mine, sign of an encroaching industrialization in this remote outpost of a pastoral past. The mere location of the mine, situated far above the city and overlooking the valley with its houses, hints at the power it wields over the people down below it. "Pointed obscenely at heaven," its phallic smokestack figures, in a sense, a modern-day replacement of a church steeple, the traditional link to Heaven that has apparently lost meaning in an industrialized world (Kingsolver 1990a: 9). The image suggests that industrialization, placed between humans and Heaven, represents a breach with past traditions and the emergence of a new set of values.

The pecan orchard, especially, provoking mixed impressions and emotions in Codi, represents the onlooker's confusion, her growing sense of being a "stranger to Grace" (Kingsolver 1990a: 12).

If you've never walked through an old orchard, you have to imagine this: it presents you with an optical illusion. You move through what looks like a hodgepodge thicket of trees, but then at intervals you find yourself at the center of long, maddeningly straight rows of trees, standing like soldiers at attention. There's a graveyard in northern France where all the dead boys from D-Day are buried. The white crosses reach from one horizon to the other. I remember looking it over and thinking it was a forest of graves. But the rows were like this, dizzying, diagonal, perfectly straight, so after all it wasn't a forest but an orchard of graves. Nothing to do with nature, unless you count human nature. (Kingsolver 1990a: 13)

Codi's suspicion of the presumable peacefulness of her environment increases as the phrase "optical illusion" indicates: while at times the orchard seems a natural "hodgepodge thicket of trees," at other times it appears lifeless, "maddening" in its human-made order and precision. Its suggestion of nature somehow traduced by artifice provokes Codi's resistance. Worse, reminding her of "soldiers at attention" and a "forest of graves," the orchard represents a deathly regimentation. Yet she recognizes that the trees are not a "forest" but an orchard—morphing into a war cemetery that denies the very possibility of fruition. The graves, then, represent the "fruit" of an emphatically human "cultivation" of death. But Codi does not, as her growing ambivalence might lead one to assume, lack family relations and friendships. She is leaving a lover behind in Tucson, and though calling herself an "orphan," she has a father who lives in Grace, a father whom she has come to see as he is old and "conceivably dying" (Kingsolver 1990a: 10). In feeling a "stranger" in a familiar landscape and in the midst of social relationships, Codi here expresses the emotional confusion that affects her very perceptions of the environment.

Early in the novel, Kingsolver suggests that Codi's bewilderment is caused not only by present impressions that merge with memory fragments but also by a basic lack of memory that, as critic Sheryl Stevenson in her discussion of the novel observes, is characteristic of trauma survivors (2001: 328).[16] For example, when arriving in Grace, Codi recognizes neither a game children play with a piñata nor her father's housekeeper, who helped raise her as a child (Kingsolver 1990a: 16, 66). Noting how amnesia shapes this narrative "of gaps, evasions, and sudden fissures of erupting emotion," Stevenson discerns the kind of "unstable discourse" that "traumatized people, pulled by conflicting impulses" produce (Stevenson 2001: 329). Indeed, growing up in Grace, Codi suffered two key traumatic experiences that eclipsed all other memories. These experiences, themselves repressed, surface in the narrative in reverse order. She reveals the more recent almost casually: "I'd come close to having a baby of my own once, but I thought of it now so rarely that the notion of myself as a mother always caught me off guard" (Kingsolver 1990a: 43). But the infrequency with which she calls to mind the lost child does not mean that she has psychologically dealt with the experience. The unexpectedness of its reemergence suggests that the painful memory lives on festering in the narrator's unconscious. Codi's overall lack of childhood memories derives from this trauma-imposed repressive mechanism, which makes her feel like "the victim of a head injury" (Kingsolver 1990a: 47).

Kingsolver encodes a more general lack of memory—the cause of a missing sense of identity—in the second traumatic experience, one an unsupportive social environment further aggravated rather than relieved. When Codi was only three years old, her mother died, making Codi and Hallie partial orphans. Never worked through, the event continued to resurface—like the unwanted pregnancy—as a feeling of memory dislocation. Worse, the existence of two conflicting stories about the death compounds the psychological damage: "According to generally agreed-upon history, Hallie and [Codi] were at home with a babysitter" (Kingsolver 1990a: 48). And yet Codi recollects in great precision the alfalfa fields surrounding the helicopter that was to take her sick mother to Tucson. She is also aware that her mother, not wanting to fly, died right there in the fields (Kingsolver 1990a: 49). She ascertains, "This is my problem—I clearly remember things I haven't seen, sometimes things that never happened. And draw a blank on things I've lived through" and concludes, "Memory is a complicated thing, a relative to truth but not its twin" (Kingsolver 1990a: 48). Codi's father, all the while, to punish her for her "fictions," as he says, forced her to read the *Encyclopedia Britannica*. The term "orphan," then, designates that Codi lost along with her mother, also her father—if only emotionally. To quote the author directly, "I wanted to write about the way that loss of memory is the loss of self, both for a culture and an individual" (Kingsolver 1990b: 3+).

More specifically, Kingsolver explores what it means for a woman to have lost both mother and daughter. "[M]y years in Grace were peculiarly bracketed by death," Codi reflects, "I'd lost a mother and I'd lost a child" (Kingsolver 1990a: 50). What makes the loss so traumatic is that it involves the closest female relatives because, as feminists have pointed out, mother-daughter relationships are central in women's lives, early and later. Critic Marianne Hirsch explains, "[P]sychoanalytic feminists take as their starting point the formative influence of the pre-oedipal period and the female parent's domination of that period. The belief in a unique bond between mother and female child leads . . . to a re-definition of maturity as different either from autonomy and separation or from self-division and alienation. Adult personality, embedded in connectedness, offers a picture of continued mother-daughter entanglement" (1989: 132).[17] The absence of a mother affects Codi's overall ability to relate to her surroundings: Without the possibility of continuing this pre-oedipal connection, Codi is unable to enter into any new meaningful relationships with the external world. Only with Hallie, to whom she was a mother replacement, does she connect deeply. Hallie, for her part, never used to having a real mother, also never suffered from losing her and thus, Codi states, "thrived anyway—the blossom of our family" (Kingsolver 1990a: 49).

Two events centrally assist Codi in regaining a sense of self, notably by compelling her to expand her vision from focus on herself to concern for her immediate environment. The initiation process involves her intellect and emotions and asks for her personal commitment. At a party, Codi learns about environmental problems in which power hierarchies in the community play a substantial role. The sturdy, much admired fruit trees, she hears, drop their unripe fruit as a consequence of the mine's poisoning the ground: "It's going to kill every damn tree in this canyon," a man affirms (Kingsolver 1990a: 64). Yet the locals, who depend on the trees for a livelihood, appear unable to do anything to prevent the "leaching operation" that pollutes the earth: "They're getting gold and moly out of them tailing piles. If they wasn't, they wouldn't keep running the acid through them" (Kingsolver 1990a: 64). The town is pitched against a politically and financially more powerful mine: "They'll pull some kind of strings" (Kingsolver 1990a: 64). Indeed, the mine merely has to "dam up the river" to fulfill EPA requirements (Kingsolver 1990a: 111). Moral and ethical considerations, Kingsolver implies, have no place in a capitalist world.

As a result of listening to the men's conversation, Codi's perception of the natural landscape changes. Her transformation from the community's outsider to insider is manifest in the language she uses: "The dead mountain range of tailings on the lip of the mine had sat for decades, washed by rain, and still was barren as the Sahara. From a distance you might guess these piles of dirt to be fragile, like a sandcastle, but up close you'd see the pinkish soil corrugated with vertical ridges and eroded to a sheen, like rock. It would take a pickaxe to dent it" (Kingsolver 1990a: 48). Metaphors of death and infertility dominate the passage and symbolize a complete shift from pastoral expectations—and projections—to an awareness of the actual land, which appears exposed, naked, and unable to regenerate after the abuse. The "ridges" that alternate with a hard, polished-looking topsoil are signs of the infertility one would expect of a "rock." Newly conscious of the damages the mine causes to the environment, Codi jettisons her romantic dream of a pre-industrial, wholesome agrarian community in favor of a more "realistic" view of the present. Being an insider, the reader understands, involves a comprehension of the "reality of the land."

This reality also includes those people who live on the land, where clear class and racial hierarchies prevail. Ultimately, these hierarchies—with white corporate America, represented by the mine's CEO, on the one hand and the town's poor minorities, who find employment in the mine, on the other—are what underlie and enable environmental despoliation. Significantly, for those who are native to the region, the destruction of nature also concurs with the annihilation of their culture. Similar to Warren and Plumwood, Kingsolver thus suggests that the loss of the land as a result of capitalist exploitation may coincide with a traumatic and dangerous loss of culture, and even of the individual's sense of self.[18] Furthermore, social hierarchies are intricately entangled with Western myth and culture forced the adjacent Navajo, Apache, and Pueblo communities off their lands. Loyd, Codi's Apache/ Pueblo friend, explains, "Gracela Canyon used to be *in* the reservation. The whites took that little section back after some guys hit gold down there" (Kingsolver 1990a: 123). Expelled from their land, the native communities do not thrive. The removal of Native Americans—a common story—exposes a cultural clash on yet another, a philosophical, level: Euro-American exploitation of the land and its native inhabitants has a twin brother in a deep unconcern for the consequences of one's actions.

The natives, by contrast, because they depend on the land for daily nourishment and are tied to it through ancestral roots and cultural traditions, reveal greater forethought than the CEOs from the big city. They know how much their lives are implicated in nature. Loyd, who deplores the commodification of the land (he refuses to call it "property"), affirms his willingness to die for the community's right to resist its destruction. To recover her sense of self, Codi has to gain an awareness of both social inequities and environmental problems and understand their underlying cultural causes.

Resistance to capitalist abuse takes two differently gendered forms in Grace.[19] Desiring to protect their fruit trees, the men in Grace choose a conservative bureaucratic route—which, in traditional society, is closed to the women—and ultimately manifest an attitude that compares with that of the dominant culture. Quite in the spirit of the traditional Western hero—a migrant who subdues and settles the land and thus brings progress to the wilderness—the men find their only solution in literally moving on. Sitting around at town meetings talking "for about nine or ten hours" with a "hotshot guy from Phoenix" (Kingsolver 1990a: 111), they seem paralyzed by fear of the mine's power where, as "crane operators" and "dynamite man," "when the mine was running," they found work, but, through it, also participated in the destruction of the land (Kingsolver 1990a: 179). Upon one woman's suggestion to use dynamite "to fix up them bulldozers" that divert their water, another woman observes, "These men don't see how we got to do something *right now*. They think the trees can die and we can just go somewhere else, and as long as we fry up the bacon for them in the same old pan, they think it would be . . . that it would be *home*" (Kingsolver 1990a: 179). The passage illustrates how the American pioneer spirit influences the men in Grace, who perceive as home not any specific place but wherever basic needs are satisfied. This attitude makes land disposable.

The women, in turn, gradually instigate a movement that ties the entire community together and reveals its direct connections with the natural environment. In opposition to the men, the women connect with nature on a variety of levels and, in some respect, even identify with it. Most importantly, though, the women stand for at once cultural continuation and adaptation to a new environment: they uphold the community's traditions and customs, which, the reader later finds out, originate in Spain: The local mascot is a peacock, and to the "Chicken Scratch music," the Papago women imitate chickens, "mov[ing] in a loose line, slightly bent over, shuffling over the gravel and sounding—if not looking—exactly like the scratching hens that give the music its name" (Kingsolver 1990a: 113). On a familial level, the land links the community to their Spanish ancestors and thus creates a sense of belonging: On All Souls' Night, all women and children go to the cemetery and decorate the graves with artificial and fresh flowers, ornaments and food. Kingsolver writes, "The unifying principle was that the simplest thing was done with the greatest care. It was a comfort to see this attention lavished on the dead. In these families you would never stop being loved" (Kingsolver 1990a: 163). To the women, the land is what provides food to feed the living; it takes the dead who through flowers and care continue to live on in spirit and in memories. In short, the land is the source of the circularity of life. Lacking the connection to both the land and her ancestors, Codi, however, feels excluded from their rites: "More than anything else I wish I belonged to one of these living, celebrated families, lush as plants, with bones in the ground for roots" (Kingsolver 1990a: 165).

Codi's estrangement goes back to her father's own alienation. Both Homer and her mother were born and grew up in Grace. Yet seeking to distance himself for social reasons (his branch of the family was considered "trash" by the villagers) (Kingsolver 1990a: 260), Homer moved to Illinois as a young man. When back in Grace and raising his children, he "canceled his ancestors" and neglected to tell Codi and Hallie about his childhood origins when teaching them that they did not belong to the community (Kingsolver 1990a: 137). The effects of this deliberate effort to erase the past, a trauma for the entire family including Homer, are manifest in the latter's compulsive behavior, his frequent experiences of time lapses that combine memories and present perceptions, and, above all, in his melancholic and obsessive desire to "photograph the past" (Kingsolver 1990a: 138): Through his photographs, Homer seeks to prove the common lineage of the town's inhabitants—at birth, when he takes their pictures, all Grace's babies' eyes are blue—a lineage that also encompasses the Nolinas (Kingsolver 1990a: 283). Through Homer, Kingsolver poses the question of what happens to those who consciously distance themselves from their culture.

Homer's erratic, trauma-driven comportment, particularly his photographic compulsion, has followed Codi all through her life. Thus, in visions, nightmares, or "eyeball dreams"—of whose origins she is oblivious—the flash he used when taking this first picture of her eyeballs appears to her persistently: "Just a sound, like popping glass, and then I'm blind. It's a very short dream" (Kingsolver 1990a: 197). In spite of Homer's intent to prove family connections in the village scientifically, this "dream" signifies Codi's loss of identity: "I understood that the terror of my recurring dream was not about losing just vision, but the whole of myself, whatever that was" (Kingsolver 1990a: 204). Paradoxically, then, what was meant to prove family ties seals Homer's own loss of self with that of his daughter.

The author suggests that if Codi wants to belong in Grace, she must recover both her cultural and personal memory. This proposition agrees with ecofeminist philosophy. For example, Warren points out that the loss of either or both undermines environmental ethics and humanist values: [20] "Cultures and cultural contexts *themselves*—the contexts in which environmental costs and benefits are analyzed, calculated, and distributed—are among the most important issues any adequate environmental ethic must address. . . . These cultural losses are *themselves* issues of environmental justice. . . . What is *also* at issue is the respectful treatment of cultures themselves—the cultural values, integrity, history, lifestyle, sustainability, and identities of the parties to the conflict" (Warren 2000: 183–84).

Codi's initiation into the past and into another culture's views of the world occurs particularly in the Pueblo town of Santa Rosalia, where her boyfriend Loyd takes her. Glimpses of the Native American community provide an alternative model of living with the land—and with the past. Contrary to Grace, Santa Rosalia does not exhibit the dualisms (between nature and culture, male and female, and dominant and minority cultures) that the novel has thus far established. Native American spirituality and ceremonies demonstrate reciprocity and respect for the land. The providing land is celebrated so that it will continue to sustain the community. This sense of connection is also evident among the townspeople, whose lives are governed by relationships and dependence, rather than autonomy or domination. Even the architecture of Santa Rosalia Pueblo illustrates these close relationships. Homes here take on the shape of the landscape:

> The village was built on a mesa and blended perfectly with the landscape, constructed of the same stones as the outcroppings that topped all the other, empty mesas. . . .. It was a village of weathered rectangles, some stacked step-wise in twos and threes, the houses all blending into one another around a central plaza. The stone walls were covered with adobe plaster, smooth and appealing as mud pies: a beautiful brown town. The color brown, I realized, is anything but nondescript. It comes in as many hues as there are colors of earth, which is commonly presumed infinite. (Kingsolver 1990a: 227)

The term "blended" signals the relationship between human and natural landscapes. Built of the same native, not imported material of which the mesa consists, the houses are a manifestation of both human adaptation to and dependence on nature for providing means of survival. The blending characteristic, in addition, may function as a protective mechanism against invading enemies. The houses' architectural replication of the mesa is paralleled in the town's overall plan with its "weathered rectangles . . . stacked step-wise in twos and threes." This design reproduces an aspect of mountain ridges that suddenly drop off to the plain, and the plain itself is echoed in the town's "central plaza," the center of community life. From afar, the settlement would thus barely be noticeable; up close, however, the onlooker detects a town full of life. This architecture not only exhibits a sure, instinctive deference to the environment, the landscape, but also facilitates a sense of community and connections among the town's inhabitants.

Santa Rosalia Pueblo appeals to just about all of Codi's senses. Tactile, olfactory, visual, and gustatory combine with her emotional sensation of connectedness to a community that has the qualities of a home: "There wasn't a soul out, but lines of smoke drifted from chimneys and the big adobe beehive ovens that squatted in every third or fourth backyard. . . . The ladders that connected one rooftop to the next were drifted lightly with snow. One house had a basketball hoop nailed to the end beams. Front curtains everywhere glowed with warm interior light, though it was still early afternoon, and strings of bright red chilies hung by the front doors" (Kingsolver 1990a: 227). Despite the chilliness of the day and the emptiness of the plaza, the scene reflects warmth, vibrancy, and connection. Unlike the small Western family units, community life means sharing in Santa Rosalia: smoke from the ovens that several families use and ladders connecting the living quarters indicate a closeness among families that protects against the harsh environment. At dinner with Loyd's family, Codi can even "taste" the affection by which she is surrounded: Through the homemade, adobe oven-cooked bread with its "hard brown crust and a heavenly, steaming interior" that, she states, "tasted like love," Codi metaphorically ingests the values that this passage so centrally marks (Kingsolver 1990a: 231). While expressions of home-making may differ from one culture to another, they all create a sense of belonging, complete with a social net, protection, affection, and cultural continuation.

Yet despite its traditional appearance, Santa Rosalia has been affected by the contemporary world. Kingsolver traces a generational split between an older populace that seeks to preserve cultural traditions and teenagers who have increasingly become Westernized. In this matrilineal culture, where the older women cut their hair in traditional style and wear silver and turquoise jewelry to "shield their knuckles," the younger jeans-wearing girls display acculturation to American mainstream culture (Kingsolver 1990a: 231).

Coming from the women—"kind of the center of things," Kingsolver writes—this type of transformation signifies a loss in the world of the novel (Kingsolver 1990a: 233).

Even so, native ceremonies play an important role in this community—and serve to suggest an alternative to the American mainstream. The author elaborates this perhaps romantic idea with a representation of Native American religious beliefs. Spirituality as transcendence of the self occupies a central position in ecofeminist philosophy because it enables a suspension "between doors"—between the self and other—that invests life with hope (Warren 2000: 196). Warren maintains that only when we comprehend our-selves as not only ecologically but also spiritually related to our surroundings will we overcome dualisms and be able to "develop earth-respectful, care-sensitive practices toward humans and earth others" (2000: 198). Similarly, Kingsolver explores Native American spirituality and its effects on human interaction with the land in such religious rites as the "corn dance" and the "eagle dance." The men who dress as deer, even move like deer, finally are the embodiment of deer: "They looked exactly as deer would look if you surprised them in a secret rite in the forest, moving in unison" (Kingsolver 1990a: 237). In a world where the spiritual and the secular are indistinguish-able, versatility and flux characterize both the corporal worlds of animals and humans, on the one hand, and a mystical world, on the other, which affects human consciousness (Kingsolver 1990a: 237).

The concept of ecological "balance," in turn, is evidenced in the meaning of the dances. Contrary to Codi's initial understanding, they are performed to celebrate not some "deal with the gods" but what the earth has provided (Kingsolver 1990a: 239); they at once symbolize and enact a certain fluctuat-ing mutuality, or reciprocity, between humans and the land—what Loyd calls a "balance" (Kingsolver 1990a: 239). Pueblo ceremonies, Kingsolver insists, preach gratefulness, which naturally inhibits misuse and abuse. "It's not like making a deal," Loyd explains, "bad things can still happen, but you want to try not to *cause* them to happen. It has to do with keeping things in bal-ance. . . . The spirits have been good enough to let us live here and use the utilities, and we're saying: We know how nice you're being. We appreciate the rain, we appreciate the sun, we appreciate the deer we took. Sorry if we messed up anything. You've gone to a lot of trouble, and we'll try to be good guests" (Kingsolver 1990a: 239). Nature is understood as a system in which everything depends on everything else—survival of one link in the system ensures the survival of another. For that reason, it is important, on departing, to leave the world as it is, without having affected radical change, for exam-ple, the decimation or extinction of species. Human respect, then, will also lead to continued offering of the earth's goods. In providing insight into the role and purpose of spirituality in Pueblo culture, Kingsolver demonstrates that relationships can exist beyond domination and oppositionality.

The celebration marks a crucial moment in Codi's journey toward self-awareness. "Entranced," she experiences a spiritual transcendence that links her with the spirits the dancers invoke (Kingsolver 1990a: 237). At the same time, she crosses an intellectual threshold, as separation from nature gives way to connection. She understands that perception of and interaction with nature are determined by culture—and may, therefore, be subject to change. As an outsider to the Native American community and also still believing in her white Illinois ancestry, Codi feels a part of the dominant culture. As such, she is also able to criticize it from within: "The way they tell it to us Anglos, God put the earth here for us to use, westward-ho. Like a special playground. . . . To people who think of themselves as God's houseguests, American enterprise must seem arrogant beyond belief. Or stupid. A nation of amnesiacs, proceeding as if there were no other day but today. Assuming the land could also forget what had been done to it" (Kingsolver 1990a: 240). Kingsolver makes an important distinction between religions and, more significantly, between our cultural interpretations of beliefs. At first she seems to suggest that religions are to be blamed for how we treat nature (or native cultures in natural spaces). Thus we refer to a Christian God who apparently not only permits but also wills the atrocities that concur with westward expansion. Nevertheless, the phrase "the way they tell it to us Anglos" hints that not God, but those who interpret His word, are at the root of our values. "American enterprise" with its "westward-ho" movement embodies the values and morals that govern mainstream America's perceptions and daily actions—for example, the conviction of being entitled to a "special playground," which to native cultures must seem "arrogant beyond belief." That last phrase contains a double meaning: Kingsolver deflates the argument that religion sanctions our way of treating the earth. Those who, as a culture, reveal such arrogance, "amnesia," "stupidity," and ignorance of the consequences of their activities on the land, she proposes, have no right to claim any kind of "belief" for moral backing. They are *beyond* belief.

As a result of the insights she gains in Santa Rosalia, Codi begins to "care." Her new attitude is manifest in a nascent environmentalism. Warren highlights an attitude of caring for and respecting the other as crucial to a transcendence of the self: "This is more than a psychological ability to empathize, since the courage involved is . . . a combination of willing and letting go, being receptive to and receiving grace" (2000: 203). To the relational self, the ability to care represents a first step toward overcoming self. "Caring" permits Codi, on the one hand, to accept and embrace what is different as an alternative way of living one's life and, on the other, to become an environmental proponent. Acting in an ecofeminist spirit "as [an] interpreter of its distress and joy," as Plumwood suggests (1997: 351), Codi, in class with her students, speaks up for nature:

> You kids think this pollution shit is not your problem, right? Somebody will clean up the mess. . . . You know how they make those [jeans]? They wash them in a big machine with this special kind of gravel they get out of volcanic mountains. The prettiest mountains you ever saw in your life. But they're fragile, like a big pile of sugar. Levi Strauss or whoever goes in there with bulldozers and chainsaws and cuts down the trees and rips the mountainside to hell, so that all us lucky Americans can wear jeans that look like somebody threw them in the garbage before we got them. (Kingsolver 1990a: 254)

Codi's speech adds a type of grassroots activism. She seeks to reach the students through a kind of vernacular appeal to their interest in fashionable clothes. Her pronouns—"you," "they," "somebody," and "us"—seem to sketch a world in which concerns of the "you" (the students) apparently do not interfere with those of the "they" and "somebodys"—those others who are supposedly the culprits, impersonal and intangible. Yet Codi strives to convey to the students something else, notably that there is no clear division between impersonal perpetrators and the innocent I (or "you"). Rather, in a capitalist society, the consumers also have a say in determining the market. Contrary to her students' self-distancing assumption that "the pollution shit is not [their] problem" and that "somebody will clean up the mess," a sense of responsibility should demand that they, the "lucky Americans," *make* it their problem.

In addition to ethics, Codi's language demonstrates her sense of aesthetics. Her own growing sense of responsibility clashes with the irresponsibility of American capitalism (embodied in Levi Strauss). With regard to the mountain, Codi rejects economic considerations in favor of what Warren calls the "loving eye," the sign of an intimate and accepting personal relationship with nature (or any other "Other") (Warren 2000: 203). Codi expresses her love for nature in phrases such as "the prettiest mountains" and "fragile, like a big pile of sugar." The fragility of the mountain makes it in need of love precisely because it also makes it vulnerable to the callousness of American capitalism that requires this purity be "cut" and "ripped to hell" with "bulldozers and chainsaws."

The heroine's grassroots activism is matched by the campaign of the women from the Stitch and Bitch Club to save Grace, a place to which they are emotionally, historically, culturally, and spiritually linked. They gain heroic stature, especially in the way they employ local customs and skills to inform the public in Tucson of their mission. Not a letter to the congressman but such domestic products as flowers, piñatas (made with local peacock feathers), and *cascarones*, sold to a "gentrified" Tucson populace, become the vehicle through which the public recognizes the problems in Grace (Kingsolver 1990a: 263). Their new fame and the money raised during the campaign permit the women to apply for Grace's landmark status.

Perhaps the key to their ultimate success lies in storytelling itself. Kingsolver indicates that cultural identification occurs through telling—remembering and celebrating—one's history. Interviewed by the local TV news station, Doña Althea begins her narrative in a ceremonious manner:

> Doña Althea lifted her head, adjusted her shawl, leaned back and put her hands on her knees, which were spread wide apart under her black skirt. "*Hace cien años,*" she began. "More than a hundred years ago, my mother and her eight sisters came to this valley from Spain to bring light and happiness to the poor miners, who had no wives. They were the nine Gracela sisters: Althea, Renata, Hilaria, Carina, Julietta, Ursolina, Violetta, Camila, and Estrella."
>
> She pronounced the names musically and slowly, drawing out the syllables and rolling the r's. They were the names of fairy princesses, but the story, in her high sustained voice, was Biblical. It was the Genesis of Grace. (Kingsolver 1990a: 267)

The "Genesis of Grace" operates as a linguistic signifier of the culture's subject position. Performance—the manner of telling the story—plays into the meaning of the town's history in a culture that sustains and celebrates its ascendance through oral transmission. Doña Althea's composed and formal posture in the chair is regal. Sitting as on a throne with her hands on her knees, she projects an image of grandeur that is quite appropriate for the town's matriarch and most direct descendant of the originators of the culture, of whom she tells. Her narrative assumes epic qualities as she chronicles the "birth" and heroics of her "civilization"—the moment when the Gracela sisters came to this area. The catalogue of foreign-sounding names and the allusion to the Bible further highlight the meaning of this foundational story to the community. In opposition to traditional epic myths, the narrative retells how not men but women performed heroic deeds to make Grace a community. She implies that the unselfish Gracela sisters sacrificed themselves to bring the miners the one thing their mining successes could not buy—"light and happiness."

The novel stipulates that a second rescue, a hundred years later, must come from within the culture. In its semblance to the present situation, the "Genesis of Grace" reveals a pattern that the novel promises to follow. Effectively, Althea's chronicle makes Codi realize that she is a part of the culture, through lineage and heritage: "[Hallie and my] father's own grandmother—mother of Homero Nolina up in the graveyard—was one of those princesses: the red-haired, feisty one" (Kingsolver 1990a: 267). Codi's overcoming her trauma and recovering a sense of identity, Kingsolver proposes, not only coincides with but also necessitates an ability to embrace a community complete with its human and nonhuman life. The community's survival, in turn, represents a parallel successful dealing with historical events—the effects of capitalist exploitation—that have caused a trauma.

Whereas the genealogical connection adds to Codi's self-assurance, she still lacks some essential information concerning the mystery of her mother's "departure." Kingsolver's insistence on Codi's recovery of her mother—a woman whom she resembles to the point that Homer, at times, mistakes her for his dead wife—makes a (pre-oedipal) mother-daughter connection central to Codi's capacity to create a home in Grace. Psychoanalysts such as Benjamin and Hirsch see this bond as necessary to nonviolent and respectful interaction with the external world, in which self and other relate through reciprocity. Benjamin observes, "The sense of responsibility promoted by the female super-ego (not the sense of separateness) curbs aggression and desire. . . . Girls learn to appreciate difference within the context of caring for others, identifying with the mother's ability to perceive the different and distinct need of others" (1988: 152).[21] The symbolic recovery of her mother through memories may permit Codi to raise her consciousness and embrace what Hirsch describes as "an alternative to patriarchy and the logos—a world of shared female knowledge and experience in which subject/object dualism and power relationships might be challenged and redefined" (1989: 133).

Kingsolver encodes this "alternative" in Codi's discovery of a new, profound love for the land, a form of "mutuality" with the Southwestern landscape itself. This love is attended by a gradually growing and clearer memory of the day of her mother's death. What further contributes is the success of the women's environmental activism, which permits Codi to invest herself emotionally in the community. After an abortive attempt to leave Grace by plane undertaken in spite—or in fear—of her growing attachment, Codi realizes:

> I laughed at myself for carrying my mother's phobic blood in my veins. . . . It seemed extraordinary and accidental that I was alive. I felt crowded with all the sensory messages that make up life, as opposed to survival, and I recognized this as something close to joy. As we slipped down over the city every building and back lot was beautifully distinct.... The land stretched out under me the way a lover would, hiding nothing, offering up every endearing southwestern cliché, and I wanted to get down there and kiss the dirt.
>
> I made a bargain with my mother. If I got to the ground in one piece, I wasn't leaving it again. (Kingsolver 1990a: 321)

Codi identifies with her mother physically—"my mother's phobic blood"— and intellectually, so that her decision for the future seals her link with the past: like her mother, who left and returned (with Homer), Codi decides to stay and thus continue, not her relationship with the real mother, but with the community of Grace, so integrated with the land itself. The novel marks her embracing all that is Grace—and a home now—with an image of reciprocated love: having given to the land and enabled its survival, Codi receives from what is now, in a posture of both offering and receptivity, "stretched out . . .

the way a lover would." Her first impulse of desiring to "get down and kiss the dirt" reinforces the idea of mutual love as Codi herself no longer can withhold her affections. Kingsolver provides a definition of life that corresponds to insights Codi has been gathering in the course of her stay in Grace, notably that life consists of details—details that, perceptible only to the attentiveness of love, involve the senses to the point that one may feel "crowded." Memories merging with the present moment signal the continuity of past, present, and a future as enabled by love. Codi's sweeping view of the landscape thus includes details of individual buildings and back lots next to thoughts about her mother. Her new "joy," then, demonstrates why "every . . . southwestern cliché" is now "endearing" to her. Being in love—even with a place—Kingsolver suggests, may feel like the "end of a depression."

The novel's closing pages convey a message of hope. Codi's pregnancy at once embodies the novel's central ecofeminist values: the remembrance of the past and one's love for the land and community make a future possible. To create a home, Kingsolver stipulates, one has to be in touch with one's roots. As daughters of mothers and mothers with daughters, women (unlike men in patriarchal, capitalist society) are capable of that blurring of the boundaries between self and other/"Other" essential to attaining reciprocity with the natural and human surroundings. Storytelling, in particular, permits women to share their female knowledge and thus replicate, in a sense, the mother-daughter relationship. The transcendence of the self through relationality ultimately also contributes to the healing of all: "We reached the crest of the canyon where the white salt crust of the old alfalfa fields began. Dead for two decades, the earth was long and white and cracked, like a huge porcelain platter dropped from the heavens. But now the rabbitbrush was beginning to grow here too, topped with brushy gold flowers, growing like a renegade crop in the long, straight troughs of the old irrigation ditches" (Kingsolver 1990a: 341). The land, thanks to the women's efforts to save Grace, shows a gradual recovery. While white salt crust points at infertility, the growing rabbitbrush announces regeneration—although, admittedly, not in the shape of pretty garden flowers or traditional crops.[22] A sturdy plant with yellow flowers in late summer and fall, rabbitbrush is a "renegade" in the sense that it refuses to participate in the fate of so much of the local flora. Despite all odds, it grows and thus ensures a future, one with new aesthetic and ethical standards: the term "gold" reflects this transformation in values, from the "gold" miners sought in the earth to the "gold" blossoms of the flower. What is desirable, then, is no longer a lucre but a living and life-giving plant, native to the soil, resilient, and adaptable. The plant's beauty lies in its significance to the regeneration of the land community.

Kingsolver figuratively addresses the question of who becomes, in the future, the "renegade" flowering amid the structures of the old and obsolete. An outsider, Codi, with the help of the women from the Stitch and Bitch

Club, is the first to prepare a future for herself and the child growing within her. This future in Grace, a place she initially was prepared to give up for lost, involves love and care for the human and natural community. Perhaps, then, the "renegade" is Codi's unborn baby, who, growing in a place that seemed hostile, embodies what is to come.

The novel discusses a woman's dream landscape as arising from an encounter with an actual landscape—an encounter that makes possible a new set of images about the land. If pioneer women enjoyed the "recognition of 'several wild vegetables' or the domestication of local flora in home gardens," as Kolodny suggests, Codi (a pioneer in her own way) learns to value native plants (1984: 49).[23] Furthermore, Codi's metaphorical "garden," as it were, emphasizes the dual need for cultural remembrance and adaptation to the local environment. Thus, Codi's new "domesticity" stresses family connections—the reconciliation with her father—and community relationships. Care, respect, and love duplicate themselves in environmental protection. "I'm teaching [the students] how to have a cultural memory," Codi states. "I want them to be custodians of the earth" (Kingsolver 1990a: 332).

In *Animal Dreams*, Barbara Kingsolver explores the relevance of the traditional male Western myth for the new millennium—and demands the myth's transformation. Unraveling the intricate connections between the individual's psychic trauma (configured in Codi's sense of dislocation at the beginning of the novel) and the historical "trauma" of capitalist exploitation (stipulating social separation from the land), Kingsolver argues that a future lies in a radical reconceptualization of social paradigms. Thus, she envisions in her ecofeminist "myth" solutions to counter these traumas. Women and marginal cultures with their capacity to "recognize" the land—in Benjamin's sense—and to experience reciprocity, she shows, provide a model for creating a future. Overcoming the dominant myth and recasting it for all those neglected "Others," then, is essential to the learning process of reader, nation, and Western culture generally. Codi's new attitude conveys what Kolodny describes as "imaginative daring" (1984: xiii). The imaginative transfiguration of a natural space symbolizes a first step toward environmental protection; change, then, springs from shifting the "paradigms in our head" (1984: xii). Ecofeminists visualize a future in which both male and female benefit from the values that the novel endorses. If culture engenders values, we can all, men and women alike, by changing our cultural archetypes, eventually achieve true mutual recognition.

> Your dreams, what you hope for and all that, it's not separate from your life. It grows right up out of it.
>
>   Loyd

NOTES

1. As Kingsolver herself has pointed out in interviews, social concerns inform all her work and give it a purpose that, she explains, must characterize any meaningful writing. As such, *Animal Dreams* is based on historical events that she recorded in her documentary *Holding the Line: Women in the Great Arizona Mine Strike of 1983* (1989). Having grown up in an impoverished part of the country, in rural Kentucky, Kingsolver feels obligated to fight for social justice (quoted in Perry 1993: 145).

2. Henry Aay discusses that, in this "ecofictional" novel, Kingsolver views "the themes of environmental degradation, conflict and restoration" in their relationship to Western myth (1993/1994: 65).

3. My reading departs from that of the few critics who also apply psychoanalytic theory to the novel: while Elizabeth McDowell (1992) uses Marcuse's concepts of Thanatos and Feminist Eros to critique the effects of modern capitalist society on the (female) psyche, I base my examination on Jessica Benjamin's explorations of object-relationships. Sheryl Stevenson, in turn, discusses how trauma, mourning, and memory loss coalesce in the novel as loss of the self, which precludes the creation of a home (2001). My own psychoanalytic reading adds to Stevenson's approach by examining the implications of traumatic losses on female consciousness.

4. While Kingsolver criticism, more generally, has concentrated on such issues as environmentalism, politics, myth-making, gender and racial concerns, writing, the quest for identity, social activism, as well as the author's biography (see, for example, Perry 1993), some critics of *Animal Dreams* focus more specifically on the author's engaging of Western myth—though other myths have also been associated with the novel: see Naomi Jacobs (2003). By contrast, Roberta Rubenstein (1996: 5–22) relates the novel to the Odyssey and the Homeric quest.

5. Jacobs describes what she perceives as the author's conscious intention: "The artist's maverick responsibility is sometimes to sugarcoat the bitter pill and slip it down our gullet, telling us what we didn't think we wanted to know" (2003).

6. Terri Moser (1999) and Vicky Newman (1995) also explore the didactic potential of the novel: Newman, for example, uses the novel as a teaching tool in the classroom. Shifting focus from the environmental issues the novel addresses, she claims that "as educators, we come to understand through this novel the importance of critically reading our histories, for it is the process of deconstructing and reconstituting personal and community histories that reveals to the protagonist of the novel—and to its readers—the importance of the role of the teacher. This process links autobiography with landscape, community, and place by revealing how history, community, and narrator are reclaimed through deconstruction and reconstitution of memory and of histories and social and ecological practices" (1995: 105). Drawing on W. J. T. Mitchell's *Landscape and Power* (2002), she asserts that landscape, then, can be read like a text. As cultural "history," it provides knowledge about racial, class, and gender relationships in the past and present that a critical—deconstructive—reading will unearth (Newman 1995: 110). Ultimately, she claims, readers (her students) will learn to position themselves vis-à-vis their own culture/ landscape through "cultural memory" (Newman 1995: 116).

7. Language must be perceptibly new and address relationships: "Unlike more traditional approaches to ethics," Warren claims, "a narrative approach contextualizes ethical discourse in ways that make relationships and beings-in-relationships central to ethics" (2000: 102).

8. Kolodny focuses especially on language that "feminizes" the wilderness (configured as "Mother" and "Virgin") as a way to reflect and heighten its desirability for the male settler (1975a).

9. More specifically, Kolodny (1975a) explores the detrimental consequences of radical separation/individuation on relationships—not only with other human beings but also with landscape. Because they could not "own" their longing for landscape, artists could, at least, make it permanent through their creative works. Hence rather than the landscape itself, art remakes the painter's desire for it. A problem arises, however, when painterly or writerly conceptions make the "real" landscape unavailable in itself, as when the desire for landscape springs from a primary loss and a latent desire for reconnection, or fusion, with the mother. Hardly limited to the longing of the occasional male settler or artist, this latency is more or less

universal. It lies behind the proliferation of "female" landscape imagery. Still, Kolodny also conceives of a reciprocal relationship between men and the land in her discussion of Faulkner's Ike McCaslin. This relationship can only work, though, if it involves a single male. Reciprocity emphasizes stewardship rather than exploitation, communality rather than ownership, control, and mastery.

10.   Feminist critique of rationality does not seek to abandon the scientific project but to redefine it by overcoming dualisms and finding relationships, the continuities between mind and nature. Benjamin observes, "The masculine stance toward difference accords with the cultural dominance of a 'science that has been premised on a radical dichotomy between subject and object.' The world outside, the other, is always object. As the first other, the mother, becomes an object, . . . her object status infuses the world and the natural environment" (Benjamin 1988: 190).

11.   To Benjamin, mutual recognition helps overcome cultural and social dualisms and leads away from aggression and self-absorption and to love and care for others because, she states, "At the heart of psychoanalytic theory lies an unacknowledged paradox: the creation of difference distorts, rather than fosters, the recognition of the other. Difference turns out to be governed by the code of domination" (1988: 135). The desire for autonomy, then, damages the boy as much as the girl because autonomy always carries domination within it.

12.   Benjamin draws on the resources of all three strands of feminist theory. Like the liberalists, she affirms equality, like the gynocentrics, she sees subjectivity as relational, and like the constructivists, she uncovers the forces that make subjectivity possible (see Steele 1997: 90).

13.   Benjamin states, "The self-obliteration of the permissive parent who cannot face this blow does not bring happiness to the child who gets everything he demands. The parent has ceased to function as an other who sets a boundary to the child's will, and the child experiences this as abandonment; the parent co-opts all the child's intentions by agreement, pushing him back into an illusory oneness where he has no agency of his own. The child will rebel against this oneness by insisting on having his way even more absolutely. The child who feels that others are extensions of himself must constantly fear the emptiness and loss of connection that result from his fearful power. Only he exists; the other is effaced, has nothing real to give him. The painful result of success in the battle for omnipotence is that to win is to win nothing: the result is negation, emptiness, isolation" (1988: 35).

14.   Crucially, constructivist feminists do not posit innate differences between masculine and feminine; difference, rather, follows a cultural script taking effect in early childhood development. Language acquisition plays an essential role in reinforcing these cultural premises. Steele states, "[Benjamin] exposes the complex process that damages men and women, and her theory can be used to critique the way our cultural narratives imprison men as well. Domination is not just a power wielded by men for their own benefit over women but a complex cultural system. She shows how feminist hermeneutics needs to go beyond pointing out bias and oppression to construct a theory of democratic subjectivity" (1997: 89–90).

15.   See also Newman: "The landscape evokes memories and these memories in turn determine how the landscape is represented" (1995: 111).

16.   Indeed, memory loss is rather a blocking out of memory. Stevenson states, "Remembering and telling the truth about terrible events are prerequisites both for the restoration of the social order and for the healing of individual victims. . . . [Yet] immense resistance to facing painful, disturbing knowledge can be seen in individuals who block out and then later recall traumatic memories" (2001: 328).

17.   Significantly, continuation does not mean identification, which would be unhealthy for the daughter or mother, but mutual recognition.

18.   In general, ecofeminists challenge all "isms of domination," that is, "oppressive conceptual frameworks," Warren explains. She cites racism, classism, ageism, anti-Semitism, heterosexism (2000: 68). "As a feminism, ecofeminist philosophy is a commitment to critique male bias wherever it occurs and to develop a theory and practice that is not male-biased. As an environmentalism, it is a commitment to critique environmental policies and decision-making structures that continue the dominations of women, other human Others, and nature, and to

develop a theory and practice which do not perpetuate interlocking 'isms of domination'" (Warren 2000: 68–69).

19. Several critics have pointed out the difference in men's and women's reactions toward environmental pollution in the novel, such as Watts (1994) and Terri Moser (1999): "Kingsolver points out that because Grace is a traditional town, it is the men, rather than the entire group, who possess the power over important town business. So the men hold a meeting with the EPA to discuss the contamination" (Watts 1994: 44).

20. Warren attributes this loss to an oppressive system (she rejects the notion that ecofeminists are inherently anti-male) with its institutional repression of women, "other human Others," and "nonhuman nature" (2000: 155). This point is significant because it provides the site where change can occur: if institutions—not individuals—represent repression, these institutions must (and can, ecofeminists hope) change: "Ecofeminist philosophy is neither inherently anti-male nor inherently pro-female. Ecofeminist philosophy is about institutional structures of power and privilege, not about praise or blame for what individuals (e.g., individual men, women, white people, upper-class people) do or do not do. . . . The focus of ecofeminist philosophy is on unjustified Up-Down systems of power and privilege, particularly patriarchal Up-Down systems, as well as on the actual social contexts in which Ups are beneficiaries of such unjustified Up-Down systems" (Warren 2000: 65).

21. Benjamin (1988) argues that girls tend to identify with rather than reject the mother—without, however, losing their autonomy. But autonomy here takes on a new meaning: self-articulation and mutual recognition within relationships rather than disconnection from all relationships. Yet a "primary identification" can be dangerous as well, she warns, because it prohibits overcoming gender boundaries. Hirsch, in turn, describes the bond as "the very basis for self-consciousness . . . a powerful mythic space, not irrevocably lost but continually present because it is recoverable in ideal(ized) female relationships" (1989: 133).

22. Rabbitbrush is one of the plants that cover erstwhile grasslands in the high plains.

23. Kolodny thus asserts that "women hailed open rolling expanses broken, here and there, by a clump of trees. In place of pristine forests, women described a cozy log cabin where 'elegantines and wood-vine, or wild-cucumber, [had been] sought and transplanted to shade the windows'" (1984: 9). In another example, humans are already included: the woman observing the natural beauty of a space is conscious of "the potential of human settlement" (1984: 37). Of course, one of the premises of *Animal Dreams* is the disappearance of the wilderness frontier, which distinguishes Codi's experience from that of pioneering women. Contrary to them, Codi does not have to make a home in pure wilderness; rather, she has to accept as a home what is already there by *adding* her own work and affections.

Chapter Three

Reintegrating Human and Nature

Modern Sentimental Ecology in Rachel Carson and Barbara Kingsolver

Richard M. Magee

When Rachel Carson's *Silent Spring* was first published in 1962, an outraged chemical industry and its constituents set out to discredit Carson's findings, and if that were not possible, to discredit Carson herself. Many of her critics charged her with sentimentality and insisted that such an emotional argument that she presented could not be scientifically sound. *Time* magazine called the book "unfair, one-sided, and hysterically over-emphatic" (Jezer 1988: 3). The subtext of *Time*'s charge clearly implies that a woman scientist is not to be trusted, that she will overreact and become emotional, that, in short, she will be "hysterical." The chemical industry that Carson's research indicts reacted no less strongly, dismissing her as part of a "vociferous, misinformed group of nature-balancing, organic gardening, bird-loving, unreasonable citizenry that has not been convinced of the important place of agricultural chemicals in our economy" (Jezer 1988: 3). The terms used to criticize and undermine Carson's argument attempt to establish a clear divide between the "reasonable" discourse of chemical companies and the "unreasonable" and "misinformed" language preferred by those who seek to balance nature. By being "nature-balancing," these citizens who drew the greatest ire of the chemical companies sought to reimagine and reconfigure the relationship of humans with the natural world so that humans and nature are no longer opposing forces but important elements of a single system.

Even more telling, however, is an irate letter received by the *New Yorker*, the only magazine willing to take the risk of publishing the work and possibly alienating readers and, worse, advertisers. The letter, from H. Davidson of San Francisco, was not originally published in the magazine but finally made it into print in the seventieth anniversary edition in 1995. After supposing that Carson most likely has "Communist sympathies," the writer asserts "[w]e can live without birds and animals, but, as the current market slump shows, we cannot live without business" (Glotfelty 2000: 158). By insisting that humans can live "without birds and animals," Davidson's letter reflects the common modernist schism where humans are viewed as separate from the natural world and are not even animals themselves. From an environmental point of view, this schism is dangerous, placing humans outside of the natural forces that govern their lives and ignoring the complex set of ecological interconnections that bind humans with their fellow living creatures. By using the language of interconnection, emotion, and feeling, Carson reintegrates human existence and the experience of the natural world along emotional and affective lines; humans thus become part of a community that includes their ecosystem instead of discrete entities who presume the non-human environment has only mechanical or pragmatic value. In *Prodigal Summer*, the novelist Barbara Kingsolver takes Carson's integration of arcadian and imperial ecology further, and clarifies the relationship to sentimental literature by crafting a narrative that is both scientifically informed and charged with emotional interrelationships symbolizing ecological interdependence. The language and tone used by both authors illustrates their reaction against a strictly mechanistic and modernistic view of nature as separate from and inferior to humans.

In his discussion of modernism and ecology, Max Oelschlaeger presents two conflicting ideologies in the human relationship to the natural world. This very structure, which suggests that humans and nature are separate, is an indication of the pervasive and problematic modernist construction of the world and the place of humans in it. Arcadian ecology, according to Oelschlaeger, is best exemplified by Gilbert White, "who moved not toward increasing scientific rigor and causal knowledge but toward an empathetic view of wild nature" (1991: 104). On the other side of the equation is imperial ecology, represented by Linnaeus, which presented a "tradition that sought the mastery of nature" and did not "recognize that humankind is part of nature" (1991: 105). Modernism supported the Linnaean mechanical model of the world (which is probably why Leo Marx's book title, *The Machine in the Garden*, is so provocative), and posited a finitely reducible, ultimately understandable, and mechanically rational universe made up of pieces with clear purposes and uses (Oelschlaeger 1991: 128). Linnaeus' modern scientific model emphasizes a mechanistic and rational paradigm that has forced us to choose between a worldview that understands nature as a living thing with which we have a "fundamental corelatedness," and a worldview that presents nature as a machine, and which "isolates [us] . . . in a silent world" (Oelschlaeger 1991: 128–29). We become isolated from nature when it becomes something in a test tube or beaker, or when it is removed from us to appear as little more than the mechanistic processes outlined in the hard sciences. The language itself is revealing: we become "isolated" and the world becomes "silent," both terms suggesting a fundamental separation from the natural world; the use of the word "silent" in the title of Rachel Carson's book further emphasizes the separation.

The history of nature writing can be seen in many ways as a history of serious attempts to ameliorate that separation and present new ways of perceiving the interconnections that complicate the human relationship with the natural world. Gilbert White's *Natural History of Selbourne*, Susan Fenimore Cooper's *Rural Hours*, and Henry David Thoreau's *Walden*, to name just three examples, all demonstrate the authors' attempts to articulate their understanding of their place within their respective environments. Each author uses his or her home as the central point from which to explore the world and reintegrate humans and nature in order to combat the sense of isolation. The desire to overcome this isolation by rediscovering a sense of connection to the natural world finds an important parallel in the sentimental literature of the nineteenth century, where sentimentalism seeks to redress isolation and detachment by exploring and emphasizing human connection through empathetic understanding; as Joanne Dobson points out, separation is the ultimate tragedy in sentimental literature (1997: 267). These three writers frequently used sentimental rhetorical tropes of attachment and community to emphasize their sense of the interconnections of the natural and human worlds.

However, by pointing out that some nature writing and nineteenth-century sentimental literature share fear of separation we run the risk of fatally undermining the goals of the nature writer because of the intense devaluation sentimental discourse has undergone in the past century and a half. Roland Barthes called the sentimental "unwarranted discourse" and contends that Modernism is the opposite of sentimental (Clark 1991: 1). Ann Douglas has argued that "the sentimental undermines the serious" (Clark 1991: 3). Sentimentalism bears, or seems to bear, connotations of weakness, frivolity, hysteria, immaturity, and runaway emotionalism, all of which are exactly the accusations fired at Rachel Carson's work. With sentimentalism's emphasis on an empathic emotional connection to other humans, it can appear to be a subversive enemy of modernity, which often looks with suspicion upon an empathy which may very well mislead with a falsely shared subjectivity. When we couple this mistrust with the aversion that science has to emotional appeals—appeals, which, after all, are not quantifiable or easily proven in the scientific method—it may border on heresy to suggest that Rachel Carson, one of the most influential scientists of the twentieth century, used sentimental tropes in her writing.

An important trend in late nineteenth-century nature writing further emphasizes the difficulties inherent in examining the sentimental rhetorical techniques in contemporary nature writing. Ralph Lutts traces the history of the so-called nature fakers, writers whose books "carried an extraordinary freight of Victorian sentiment and gushing, syrupy prose that left many of their authors open to serious criticism" (Lutts 1990: 172). Again, this critique of the nature-writing prose echoes in many ways the critique of Carson's work: the language invests too much emotion and not enough rational thought in attempts to sway readers to a suspect point of view. However, as Lutts further points out, the nature lovers who wrote passionately, if a little too gushingly, of their experiences in the natural world did provide an important corrective to the rational-mechanistic view of nature as they "gave voice, though sometimes in a faltering and poorly conceived manner, to a new relationship between humans and nature" (Lutts 1990: 173).

Despite the claims that the sentimental is weak or somehow flawed, such writing does present a formidable argumentative strategy by employing the readers' emotions as a link between the textual world and the world the reader inhabits. This link also partly ameliorates one of the weaknesses that "traditional nature writing" holds for modern readers. As Lawrence Buell points out in *Writing for an Endangered World*, traditional nature writing, with its emphasis on the exemplary landscape, tends toward the "downplay if not the exclusion of social justice concerns" (2001: 230). When traditional nature writing extols the beauty of, for example, a Yosemite sunrise, it perpetuates the nature/culture divide by presenting a pristine landscape untouched by human hands as somehow the only model for environmental concern. Such thinking, moreover, elides the social realities of this model of environmental concern: that elites, usually white males, work for the preservation of exemplary landscapes while ignoring the problem of something less aesthetically pleasing, such as, for example, South Bronx air pollution.

In the sentimental ecological model of nature writing, the human concerns are not ignored, but are presented as parallel to, and inseparable from, the concerns of nonhuman nature. The central human concern is community. William Shutkin, an environmental lawyer and activist, writes about what he calls "civic environmentalism" in *The Land that Could Be*. He sees parallels between the "rise in economic and social inequality" and "the deterioration of the American environment, both built and undeveloped" (2000: 3). For Shutkin, the most important force for change is community-based environmental action (2000: 13–14). Furthermore, according to Buell, "contemporary ecopopulism" is most notable for the inclusion, even the leadership, of "nonelites" who emphasize community. The community mindedness creates an "'anthropocentric' emphasis on environmentalism as instrument of social justice as against an 'ecocentric' emphasis on caring for nature as a good in itself" (Buell 2001: 33).

Rachel Carson's book created a new environmental awareness precisely because it reimagined a new connection between humans and nature, and it frequently presented this new vision using sentimental language. The first and most obvious sentimental trope in the book is the title. Paul Brooks, the Houghton editor, recalls a letter from a woman whose property had been sprayed with insecticide, killing off all of the birds; she missed their songs. Brooks suggested that the chapter about the effects of insecticide on birds be called "Silent Spring." When the publishers had trouble coming up with a title for the whole book, Brooks thought that "metaphorically, *Silent Spring* applied to the book as a whole" (2000: xvi). The title is not scientific—a more scientific title would probably be something like *The Effects of Chlorinated Hydrocarbon Insecticides on the Environment*—but it nevertheless has a powerful emotional resonance while referring to one of the central concerns of the book. Significantly, the title also reflects the silence that reigns, in Oelschlaeger's formulation, when humans are viewed as separate from or alien to the natural environment.

The opening of *Silent Spring* introduces the sentimental tropes that Carson uses with such effectiveness, and it also establishes the central conceit that is reflected in the book's title. "There was a strange stillness," Carson writes in the middle of the first chapter, which serves as a simple introduction to the complex science that comes later. She continues, "The birds, for example—where had they gone? . . . only silence lay over the fields and woods and marsh" (Carson 1962: 2). The silence of the title is the deathly silence that pervades after all of the birds had been killed by the overuse of pesticides and other agricultural and domestic chemicals that escape into the environment and cause damage far beyond what the makers first imagined. By using the birds' fate as a metaphor for humans' fate, Carson reaches past the cliché of the canary in the coal mine to the domestic iconography that informed the work of some sentimental authors. The birds are not just what biologists call "indicator species," but are metonymically connected to humans. Just as a sentimental writer might look at bird nesting in the eaves and see a model of domestic harmony and industry, Carson looks at the silencing of the birds as a frightening harbinger of our own possible fate. A reader's sympathy toward the birds is partly based upon a sense of shared experience or empathy, a central aspect of the sentimental ethos.

Many of the examples that Carson uses to illustrate her claims about the dangers of chlorinated hydrocarbon poisons come from a meticulously noted list of sources. The list of sources covers fifty-five pages at the end of *Silent Spring*, and includes several hundred articles from scientific and medical journals as well as popular mass-market magazines. Carson "borrows" the language of these sources in a Bakhtinian sense by paraphrasing and even quoting (Harris 2000: 127). The "borrowing" or paraphrasing is necessary in many cases to make unfamiliar or highly specialized language more accessible to a general audience. Carson's style is marked by "focusing emotion" and "increasing the strength of claims and instilling drama," all of which are "extremely common when material moves into public discourse from the more tentative and qualified world of scientific literature" (Harris 2000: 134). The important qualification remains that Carson does not manufacture claims or statistics. Instead, her tactic, which infuriated the chemical industry, is to manage the emotional potential of the scientific findings by carefully choosing language with greater pathos. As Randy Harris puts it, she "manages the pathos; she does not exploit it" (2000: 134).

Harris also points out some of the specific techniques Carson uses to manage the pathos she invokes. Carson describes a poisoning case that occurred when a "year-old child" had been taken to Venezuela by his parents where they encountered cockroaches in their new home. The cockroaches were killed with a spray containing the chlorinated hydrocarbon endrin, while the child and the family dog were taken out of the house. When they returned, after the floors were washed, the dog quickly sickened and died, and the baby went into convulsions and a comatose state. The baby was taken back to New York, where doctors held out little hope of recovery (Carson 1962: 27). The anecdote is powerful, with many elements—the dog's death, the child's convulsions and vomiting—that could have a strong emotional effect on the readers.

Carson's source for the story was Harold Jacobziner and H. W. Raybin's article "Poisoning by Insecticide (Endrin)" in *New York State Journal of Medicine*, published May 15, 1959. Randy Harris traces the long path the language took from the original to Carson's recounting. The authors of the article were not the attending physicians, so they are paraphrasing that doctor, who in turn must have been paraphrasing (and perhaps even translating) language from the site of the poisoning, Venezuela. However, Carson's paraphrase is the most revealing. While the authors of the medical report use the term "exposure" to discuss the patient's contact with the poison, Carson uses the term "fateful contact." Throughout the medical report, the child is referred to as an "infant," a "child," or a "patient." Carson, on the other hand, frequently uses the much more emotionally resonant term "baby" (Harris 2000: 134). Before telling the story of the dead child, Carson states that endrin has been responsible for a number of animal deaths and has also endangered human lives (Carson 1962: 27). Why then use this particular story to illustrate the dangers of the chemical, when there are, presumably, other stories? The answer is simple: it is about family, the sentimental staple, and stories about poisoned cattle do not have the same empathetic potential as stories about poisoned family dogs and babies. She chose the story for its impact and chose her language for the same reason: a domesticated story will hit her readers with a greater emotional impact and perhaps elicit more attention.

The image of the dead or suffering child is, moreover, an important trope in sentimental literature because of the salvific qualities the image implies.

Part of the power the suffering child image wields derives from the innocence and powerlessness implicit in childhood. The baby that suffers from toxic chemicals had no power to escape the danger, nor was the child responsible for the original distribution of the chemical. Because the child is innocent and pure, the pathos of the situation is magnified. Just as importantly, the child's innocence lends a redemptive quality to the illness. In its weakness and innocence, the child suffered from the pesticide use so that the adults might be saved—perhaps redeemed—and learn from the tragedy of the dangers of certain household chemicals. Without explicitly mentioning religious motivations in any way, Carson implicitly links her example to the evangelical Christian underpinnings of sentimental literature through the Christ-like suffering child.

Rachel Carson's legacy to the modern American environmental movement has been exhaustively identified, and few, if any, writers of environmental literature after 1962 can avoid her influence. Barbara Kingsolver, whose writing is frequently informed by environmental issues, makes no attempt to escape the Carson legacy in her novel *Prodigal Summer*. Instead, she names a character Rachel Carson Rawley, creates another character who embodies Carson's enlightened approach to agriculture, and digresses often to lecture her readers on environmental and ecological issues that would have interested Carson. Finally, and most important for this discussion, Kingsolver structures her narrative around a rural community and several women who personify several ecological concerns, and she does this by deploying nearly all of the expected sentimental tropes. In some ways, *Prodigal Summer* exemplifies modern sentimental ecology and its attempts to reintegrate humans and nature.

The theme of ecological and sentimental interconnectedness is immediately evident by the overall structure of Kingsolver's novel. She interweaves three plots: "Predators," "Moth Love," and "Old Chestnuts." Each plot deals with a female protagonist and a male antagonist, where the female character represents an enlightened environmental understanding and the male character usually represents a reactionary and hubristic anti-environmental stance; to use the terms mentioned earlier, the women are arcadian ecologists while the men are imperial ecologists. The three plots are interconnected by various family connections and other rural community ties. Although the book is flawed by its too-neat juxtaposition of ecological woman and toxic man and its frequent preachy digressions, it does create a vibrant fictional universe and a forum for considering ecological issues.

Kingsolver's book fits well into a number of the constructs outlined in modern ecofeminism. All of the main female characters clearly represent nature, and the men represent (agri)culture, similar to the formulation Sherry Ortner (1974) critiques in her important work. Not only do the women represent nature, but they also represent different stages of nature. Deanna is the primitive, maternal (by the end of the novel she discovers she is pregnant), and primal earth-goddess. Nannie Rawley is the old woman with the lifetime of natural folk wisdom stored up in her head. Lusa is the modern, educated woman who uses her intelligence as well as her fierce determination and family attachments to become a more ecologically sensitive farmer than any of the men who farm around her could hope to be.

The two main themes of *Prodigal Summer* are closely related. Kingsolver stresses the ecological interconnectedness of all life, and the biological imperative toward species survival. In her view, these two elements point toward sex. Procreation is the first, middle, and last purpose of nature, and thus a lavish—or prodigal—amount of energy is devoted to this end. Several times in the early scenes of the novel, Deanna notices how explosively nature works to perpetuate species. She thinks the "extravagant procreation" that she is witnessing "could wear out everything in its path with is passionate excesses, but nothing alive with wings or a heart or a seed curled into itself in the ground could resist welcoming it back when it came" (Kingsolver 2000: 51). The "passionate excesses" of nature struggling to reproduce means that different species become connected to and dependent upon each other. In trying so hard to reproduce, an oak tree produces thousands more acorns than can reasonably grow in an area, but this prodigality means that wildly reproducing mice have something to eat and feed their young, which, in turn, means that predators, such as Deanna's beloved coyotes, have something to eat and feed their young.

Kingsolver develops two distinct yet related themes of interconnection: ecological and social or sentimental. The ecological interconnections run throughout the novel and often reflect the impact that human intervention has on the ecosystem. Several times Kingsolver describes the problem of cockleburs, a plant whose seeds grow in burs that cling tenaciously to everything they touch, especially the pants and socks of unsuspecting hikers. At one point, Garnett wonders to Nannie why God created so many cockleburs and speculates that he may have gotten carried away in his enthusiasm for the nuisance plant (Kingsolver 2000: 219, 335). He triumphantly tells Nannie, who has argued that human meddling has created many of the pest problems, that he, and by extension, other farmers, cannot be blamed for the cocklebur problem (Kingsolver 2000: 336). Garnett, though, is wrong. Deanna calls the burs "parakeets' revenge," because the burs were once the favorite food of the Carolina parakeet, and the two species—predator bird and prey plant— had coevolved to form a complex balance. The Carolina parakeet had been hunted to extinction very soon after settlers arrived in the Appalachians, and the cockleburs, with no natural predator, proliferated at a great rate. The plants, Deanna wryly thinks, were "trying to teach a lesson that people had forgotten how to know" (Kingsolver 2000: 247). The lesson, of course, is that the balance of predator and prey in an ecosystem is incredibly complex, and ignorant human meddling can wreak serious havoc on that balance.

Traditional nineteenth-century sentimental literature frequently employed a strong evangelical Christian theme, and the young heroines of these works generally found redemption or comfort in biblical teachings. The case in Kingsolver's modern take on the sentimental is more complicated than that, and further illustrates the problems inherent in the modernist reduction to clear binaries that separate humans from the natural world. The human/nature dichotomy finds a parallel in the science/religion battle that informs so much of the public debate in our society. Kingsolver, however, demonstrates as Stephen Jay Gould argues, that science and the humanities (which include religion in Gould's formulation), while composing non-overlapping magisteria, nevertheless act in the "service of a common goal" (Gould 2003: 8).

The most obvious conflict between science and religion appears clearly in an exchange between Nannie and Garnett. Garnett, the self-described "scholar of creation science," had ridiculed Nannie's belief in evolution, or, in his words, "put [her] straight on that" (Kingsolver 2000: 277). To refute his argument in favor of creation science, Nannie points out that Garnett himself is involved in a bit of *un*-natural selection in his attempts to cross breed a blight-resistant strain of chestnut tree. Garnett agrees that he is performing artificial selection in his breeding program, but he notes that he is not creating a new species, saying that only God can "make a chestnut into an oak" (280). Nannie's triumphant reply to this is that Garnett could perform this feat of evolution if he "had as much time as God does" (Kingsolver 2000: 280).

For Nannie, God has become a metaphor for the evolutionary process. She argues that the difference between Garnett's chestnut-breeding program and evolution is that Garnett has a goal in mind, while in nature "it's predators [or] a bad snap of weather" that make decisions about which organism or species will survive and which will die (Kingsolver 2000: 280). The pantheistic view of nature greatly disturbs Garnett, who cannot conceive of living in a world of "godless darkness" where there is no plan, only blind chance. The "glory of an evolving world" is, in Nannie's eyes, the transcendent experience that obliterates the darkness Garnett fears. Her sense that she is "part of a bigger something" equates with Garnett's religious beliefs, but the bigger something is not an anthropomorphic God but a huge and intricately structured web (Kingsolver 2000: 277).

Nannie believes in natural selection, but when she refers to the "glory of an evolving world," she conflates evolution (which implies progress) with natural selection (which does not). While she is conflating the terms, she is essentially saying that this big process is so awe-inspiring that it is almost like God and therefore glorious. Darwin's ideas are simplified and become metaphorical; "evolution" stands in for the whole process of natural selection, even on the level of the individual, let alone the species level. Her language, though, is anything but simple. By juxtaposing her scientifically informed views of evolution with elevated and evocative language, she links the emotional and spiritual longings of the human and the impersonal forces of natural processes, thus rhetorically reintegrating the apparent dichotomy of human and nature.

In one of the other plotlines of the novel, Kingsolver describes the dilemma Lusa, the young widow faces: she wishes to keep the family farm she inherited when her husband, Cole, died, but, because of her moral objections, she does not wish to farm tobacco. Cattle farming, though not morally repugnant to her, is too labor-intensive and difficult for her to do on her own. Complicating matters is Lusa's background: she is a trained entomologist not a farmer. Her family background, though, does come to her rescue. The product of an Arab mother and a Polish Jewish father, Lusa is comfortable navigating the antagonisms of the traditionally opposed religious spheres. This unusual background helps her find a sustainable, ecological, and morally acceptable solution to her problem. One of her mother's cousins is a New York City butcher who supplies milk-fed kid goats and sells many of them around religious holidays, and Lusa realizes that she could supply goats for Id-al-Adha, Orthodox Easter, and Passover, hitting the trifecta of Abrahamic festivals. Her scientific mind, her religious sense, and her family background all contribute to her ability to devise the scheme, follow through, and make it successful.

Kingsolver thus challenges the simple dichotomy of science and religion. Instead of separating the two magisteria and building an impenetrable wall around each, she allows the two sides to create a dialogic where their similarities reinforce each other and their differences create the friction that leads to more complex inquiry. When Nannie points out to Garnett that he is, in a small way, doing what evolution or God does, she is opening the doors to discussion rather than turning her back and refusing to countenance the old man's stubborn beliefs. Similarly, Lusa's unorthodox plan illustrates how human needs—her own need for economic stability and the religious communities' need for fresh goat—can combine with nature for mutual benefit. In Lusa's case, her understanding of science and her feelings for religion allowed the crucial dialogic to transform her previous way of thinking.

Kingsolver structures the novel so that the human community and the nonhuman environment overlap, calling into question the very notion of separate human and nonhuman ecosystems. The first chapter of the novel begins with the description of an unnamed character walking through the forest. Immediately, Kingsolver questions the assumption of anthropocentrism by responding to the initial statement of the character's solitude: "But solitude is only a human presumption" (Kingsolver 2000: 1). She goes on to note that quiet footsteps are not so quiet to the small organisms that live on the forest floor. For the first several pages, Kingsolver continues in the detached, scientific, and analytical manner of a field report describing the movements of a specimen. All of her observations point out that human activity is not the center of the world, and, furthermore, that human observation is flawed. If a "man with a gun" had been watching this character (who turns out to be Deanna), he would have thought her "an angry woman on the trail of something hateful" (Kingsolver 2000: 1). This, Kingsolver quickly tells us, is the wrong interpretation, the sort of misunderstanding, she implies, that informs so much of human interaction with the environment.

The opening description is made more remarkable by the manner in which Kingsolver returns to her theme at the end of the novel. The final chapter begins with a similar description of an unnamed "she" walking on the edges of fields that border the forest. Like Deanna in the first chapter, this female is intent on seeing, smelling, and experiencing the forest, but we quickly realize that this description is much more detailed, more earthy than the first, and it soon becomes clear that this "she" is a female coyote. The penultimate paragraph returns to the notion of the speculative "man with a gun" who might be watching the coyote. This man might believe that he and the coyote are "the only two creatures left here in this forest of dripping leaves" (Kingsolver 2000: 444). Like the hypothetical observer in the beginning, this man is wrong: "Solitude is a human presumption," Kingsolver reiterates. Everything is connected, an "impalpable thread on the web." In Kingsolver's view, all connections, including those emotional and familial connections termed sentimental as well as those between predator and prey, are inseparable parts of the ecosystem.

Rachel Carson and Barbara Kingsolver were both trained as scientists and may be expected to embrace the rationalist, mechanical view of nature as something separate from, and perhaps even inferior to, the world of humans. Yet these two women both promoted a more complex approach to modernism's scientific paradigm in which nature is not merely a separate entity for dispassionate study but also an integral part of the human community. Both women display in their rhetorical choices a keen understanding of the language of community and interconnection, and their language and writing styles constantly promote the reintegration of humans and the natural world.

Chapter Four

Shifting Subjects and Marginal Worlds

Revealing the Radical in Rachel Carson's Three Sea Books

Marnie M. Sullivan

Rachel Carson was a popular author who had been writing for the public for nearly thirty years prior to the publication of *Silent Spring* in 1962. From the earliest examples of her writing, she urged readers to respect "those with whom we share the world" and recognize both "our interdependence and the value and glory of all life" (Gartner 1983: 117). Carson purposefully wove a web to link "all creatures of the earth into one harmonious and mutually necessary existence," and this "sense of connectedness" was a guiding principle behind all her work (McCay 1993: 23). With the publication of *The Sea Around Us* (1951), Carson drew sustained attention from literary critics, scientists, and the reading public. It sold over 200,000 copies in less than a year, remained on the *New York Times* best-seller list for eighty-six weeks, and was translated into thirty-three languages (Proctor 1995: 48). The popularity of *The Sea Around Us* led to renewed interest in Carson's first book, *Under the Sea-Wind*. A second edition was published in 1952 and it joined *The Sea Around Us* on the best-seller list.[1] Carson's third book, *The Edge of the Sea* (1955), was greeted with similar enthusiasm and appeared on the best-seller list for twenty-three weeks. None of the sea books have ever been out of print. According to Mary McCay (1993: ix), the sea was Carson's primary focus and finally her greatest symbol. McCay identifies its "creative power and destructive force, its magnitude and infinite variety" that attracted Carson, as it had Melville and Conrad, and like those earlier writers, the "ocean became the medium through which Carson spoke to the world" (1993: ix). Literary critics have effectively situated Carson within Western

canons and patriarchal traditions.[2] Feminists and environmentalists have successfully documented the importance of her work. The public has celebrated
her achievements with schools, parks, and awards named in her honor.
Nevertheless, we have missed significant opportunities to investigate how
Carson's work challenges Western hegemony and have underestimated the
radical lessons cloaked in her work. Carson's three sea books were closest to
her heart, best represent a culmination of her life's work, and most clearly
demonstrate the social, political, and ethical implications of her writing.

In the sea books, as in *Silent Spring*, Carson uses literary devices in order
to translate complex scientific and technical information for a large, diverse
audience of readers. Unlike *Silent Spring*, the sea books are not organized as
arguments, and are not particularly controversial in content. Instead, these
works synthesize findings from the vast reservoir of scientific research conducted from the early twentieth century through World War II, with interrelated piquant narratives based largely on patient, low-impact observation.
Carson's formula yields surprisingly radical results. Indeed, the sea books
surpass *Silent Spring* in their preoccupation with life in the margins, satura-
tion with ambiguity, and the social and political implications associated with
these conditions. The title of each book refers to interstitial spaces that pre-
dict Carson's preoccupation with borderlands. *The Edge of the Sea* opens
with a chapter called "The Marginal World," where the pages that follow are
detailed depictions of borders, border life, and border crossers. Carol Gartner
(1983: 69) addresses Carson's attention to borders, and claims that the border
zone, "where sea meets land, where life emerged from the sea in the course
of its leisurely evolution" is where Carson compels readers to "realize that
human beings are no longer of central importance." Decentering human perspective is a strategy that resonates powerfully for ecofeminists because it is
a first step toward relating to the "other"—whether human or nonhuman
nature—as a subject. Moreover, Carson's persistent preoccupation with marginal landscapes and their inhabitants model patterns of engagement with the
"other" that fosters an ethic of care that avoids domination or exploitation.

For Carson, the edge of the sea is an elusive and indefinable boundary
with a "dual nature," where on one day "a little more land may belong to the
sea, tomorrow a little less" (Carson 1955: 1). Dualities blend and boundaries
between land and sea blur so that subjects, whether life form or landscape,
become indistinguishable one from another. On the night of the flood tide in
Under the Sea-Wind, both "water and sand were the color of steel overlaid
with the sheen of silver, so that it was hard to say where water ended and
land began" (Carson 1941: 3). The blurring of boundaries between elements
suggests the ambiguities inherent in the interaction between discrete entities.
At the same time, attention to ambiguities signal the reconciliation of elements separated by difference. For example, the "black inscription" of micro-
plants written on the shore is "the sign of the meeting of land and sea," and it

is a sign that is "the same all over the world—from South Africa to Norway and from the Aleutians to Australia" (Carson 1955: 47). Despite the appearance of unfathomable difference and the illusion of complete separation, Carson describes the unifying affect of the sea in *The Sea Around Us* where there is "no water that is wholly of the Pacific, or wholly of the Atlantic, or of the Indian or the Antarctic. The surf that we find exhilarating at Virginia Beach or at La Jolla today may have lapped at the base of Antarctic icebergs or sparkled in the Mediterranean sun" (Carson 1951: 147). There are social and political implications of Carson's engagement of borders and her regular reliance on fluidity over rigidity in descriptions of beings and landscapes in the sea books. While I am not suggesting that Carson intentionally promoted radical criticism of social, political, and economic systems prior to *Silent Spring*, I do propose that, like Charles Darwin who recognized hierarchical patterns of domination in natural systems that reflected social and political conditions of his time, Carson was drawn to natural systems that displayed patterns of interaction that were familiar to her.[3]

Borders and border crossing resonate powerfully for feminists, ecofeminists, and others in progressive movements. According to Susan Stanford Friedman (1998: 3), whether literal or figurative, material or symbolic, border talk has become a powerful concept for scholars across disciplines. Gloria Anzaldúa's (1987) collection *Borderlands/La Frontera: The New Mestiza* was among the first to explore the theoretical implications of borders, border crossing, and border culture, and to suggest the potential of border metaphors to reimagine identity, representation, and access to power. For Anzaldúa, the border is a real place with geopolitical implications, and she invokes imagery similar to Carson's when she chooses the edge of the sea as a metaphor in the generative poem that opens the work.

Borders make visible descriptions of identity in terms of dualisms of what is/is not. For Friedman, identity in a Western sense is "unthinkable without some sort of imagined or literal boundary" (Friedman 1998: 3). Val Plumwood's (1993: 31) observation that such boundaries are neither neutral nor arbitrary, rather the result of a process "by which contrasting concepts . . . are formed by domination and subordination and constructed as oppositional and exclusive" remains relevant. The by now familiar binaries of Western thinking—culture/nature, male/female, mind/body, reason/emotion, human/nature (nonhuman), production/reproduction (nature), public/private, subject/object, self/other—remain intact, and the qualities (actual or supposed) associated with the condition of being a man (for example) are culturally construed as superior, whereas the condition of being a woman is understood as inferior (Plumwood 1993: 43). Carson's descriptions of borders, border life, and border crossers portray powerful, prefeminist privileging of difference that can be understood as critiquing oppressive ideologies and patriarchal social structures.

Ecofeminist literary critics such as Karla Armbruster (1998: 106) have borrowed from feminism and poststructuralism in order to explore the ways a text conveys subjectivity as "socially and discursively constructed, multiply organized, and constantly shifting" as well as the ways a text can avoid "reinscribing dualism and hierarchical notions of difference." Indeed, for Gretchen Legler (1997: 228), reimagining what nature is and what kinds of relationships can exist can contribute to "the elimination of institutionalized oppression on the basis of gender, race, class, and sexual preference and part of what may aid in changing abusive environmental practices." Finally, Patrick Murphy and Patricia Yaeger find value in literature of the environment that challenges hegemonic constructions of nature or human relationships with nature, particularly those that promote "emancipatory strategies" that can change the way humans relate to the natural world and to each other (Legler 1997: 230). By rendering life in layers, Carson offers readers the opportunity to reflect on the conditions and consequences of a social world stratified by gender, race, class, sexual orientation, and other differences.

The sea books are imbricated with an incredibly flexible network of absolute specificity and extreme ambiguity in the demarcation of borders and zones. The edge of the sea includes both indeterminate spaces and spaces clearly discernable by difference. Of the geographic provinces of the ocean—the continental shelves, slopes, and the floor of the deep sea—Carson claims that each "is as different from the others as an arctic tundra from a range of the Rocky Mountains" (Carson 1951: 58–59). Later, she explains that the foundations of the continents are separated by bands of differently colored mud (Carson 1951: 80). On the way to her own stretch of shore in Maine, Carson differentiates land from sea by the color of the rocks beneath the forest's edge. Rocks that belong to the land are not only dry, but white or gray or buff (Carson 1955: 46). The place where the continent ends and the true sea begins between the Chesapeake Capes and Cape Cod is marked not by the distance from shore, but by a significant drop in the depth of water (Carson 1941: 109). Detectable to human senses or not, changes "from zone to zone may be abrupt. It may come upon us unseen, as [a] ship at night crosses an invisible boundary line" (Carson 1951: 20). Transitions may be extreme in addition to abrupt. For example, trawls descending through hundreds of fathoms of water pass "from ice and sleet and heaving sea and screaming wind to a place of warmth and quiet, where fish herds [browse in] blue twilight, on the edge of the deep sea" (Carson 1941: 254). A natural landscape intersected by boundaries both permeable and impenetrable is evocative of social settings constructed of multiple private and public spheres that sometimes overlap, and other times chafe. To this topography, Carson integrates communities that are similarly stratified in layers.

Carson's broad descriptions of borders and zones serve as an organized backdrop to a great diversity of social systems as well as interactions between the living and their environment. Carson observes that sea creatures "are often assorted in layers, one above another" (Carson 1941: 138) and in the mossy turf of the tide zone, "life exists in layers, one above another; life exists on other life, or within it, or under it, or above it" (Carson 1955: 95). In deeper waters, Carson describes existence this way:

> The young eels lived in one layer or tier of a whole series of horizontal communities that lay one below the other, from the nereid worms that spun their strands of silk from frond to frond of the brown sargassum weed floating on the surface to the sea spiders and prawns that crawled precariously over the deep and yielding oozes of the floor of the abyss. (Carson 1941: 260)

These layers demonstrate Carson's vision of interrelated communities, but they also suggest her sensitivity to social patterns of division and inclusion, of access and denial. In "The Pattern of the Surface," Carson notes that, "[u]nmarked and trackless though it may seem to us, the surface of the ocean is divided into definite zones, and the pattern of the surface water controls the distribution of its life" (Carson 1951: 20). Of the low water line along the coast of Maine during the lowest spring tides, Carson asserts that "although little else lives openly in this zone, thousands of sea urchins do" (Carson 1955: 108). Later, she ponders the perplexing patterns of urchins:

> For some inscrutable reason, these rock-boring urchins and related species in other parts of the world are bound to this particular tidal level, linked to it precisely and mysteriously by invisible ties that prevent their wandering farther out over the reef flat, although other species of urchins are abundant there. (Carson 1955: 214)

Carson understood that the mysterious reasons for the precise division of urchin habitat could eventually be revealed by science; however, she also suggests that limitations of human senses may always prevent us from perceiving barriers that significantly impact others. This is in conflict with the trend among many scientists who write for the public, as well as nature writers, past and present, who find in nature patterns of organization that reinforce domination of humans over nature, men over women, white people over people of color, and so forth.

Attention to the diversity of social patterns allow Carson to carefully explore the conditions of lives lived in layers and zones. Boundaries can highlight differences, and they can obscure connections. Boundaries can be penetrated, traversed, or unyielding. In *The Sea Around Us* Carson notes that "the boundary between water masses of different temperatures or salinities is often a barrier that may not be passed by living creatures" (Carson 1951: 130) and as temperatures drop during the change of seasons, increasing cold can be like "a wall moving through the sea across the coastal plane. It [is] nothing that could be seen or touched; yet it [is] so real a barrier that no fish [can] run back through it any more than if it [was as] solid as stone" (Carson 1941: 252). Carson reports on mullet "bursting through the surface film of the fish's world and falling back again like raindrops—first denting, then piercing the tough skin between air and water" (Carson 1941: 95). Borders can be mercurial and access might be discriminating, temporary, or intermittent. In a cave along the coast and through "the same openings that admit light, fish come in from the sea, explore the green hall, and depart again into the vaster waters" (Carson 1955: 118), and sand dollars, or keyhole urchins, pass "with effortless ease from the world of sunlight and water" to dim regions of which her own (human) senses know nothing (Carson 1955: 138). Here, during a rare moment when she inserts herself into the narrative, Carson privileges the perspective of the sea creature that crosses borders.

That living in layers in the natural world might reflect realities similar to those living in a world stratified by gender, race, class, sexual orientation, and other identities can be seen most clearly in Carson's sea books, in depictions of creatures confined to zones and descriptions of terrifying consequences for transgression. Fish alarmed by predators from below may dash to the surface and leap through the "strange element beyond," but in so doing, they may be seized by hovering gulls (Carson 1941: 133). Similarly grim, after a day of fishing, "bodies of the young fish—too small to sell, too small to eat—litter the beach above the water line, the life oozing from them for want of means to cross a few yards of dry sand and return to the sea" (Carson 1941: 103–4). Some have read this scene as evidence of an early critique by Carson of human abuse in the natural world; however, the dominant impression relates to the consequence of transgression, not predation. Carson's passive voice further suggests a subtle indictment of systems, rather than individual actions. Elsewhere, Carson observes similar carnage in bodies laid out in beach flotsam where "strays from the surface waters of the open ocean, [are] reminders of the fact that most sea creatures are prisoners of the particular water masses they inhabit" (Carson 1955: 164–65). These passages reveal a deep attentiveness on Carson's part to broad as well as specific penalties for overstepping boundaries. These are important lessons for all members of human society: for those restricted by geographic, economic, or social barriers, for those who cross multiple sectors, as well as for those who enforce the borders between.

The threat of sanction and violence was real for people who overstepped social boundaries in Carson's time—as well as in ours. Legler claims that writers who erase or blur boundaries between "inner (emotional, psychological, personal) and other (geographic) landscapes" encourage readers to erase or blur "self-other (human/non-human, I/Thou) distinctions" (Legler 1997: 230). By blurring such distinctions, Carson transforms the inhabitants of a bleak and oppressive zone in a fascinating manner:

> For most creatures, groping their way endlessly through [the] black waters [of
> the abyss], it must be a place of hunger, where food is scarce and hard to find,
> a shelterless place where there is no sanctuary from ever-present enemies,
> where one can only move on and on, from birth to death, through the darkness,
> confined as in a prison to his own particular layer of the sea. (Carson 1951: 39)

This passage begins with the perspective of the "other" in the form of nonhuman nature, before shifting to a more intimate "one." While "one" can be
understood ambiguously as I/Thou, the final "he" cannot. Some critics have
claimed that Carson's commitment to correct grammar governed her use of
pronouns, however, it is more accurate to argue that Carson avoided using
gendered language. The evolution from ambiguity to gendered specificity in
the passage suggests that "he" can be both dominator and dominated.

Similarly, and with less ambiguity, Carson explains that fishes of the deep
sea "may sometimes wander out of the zone to which they are adjusted and
find themselves unable to return" (Carson 1951: 49). In painfully slow, blow-
by-blow bursts, she describes how a fish roaming as it feeds might acciden-
tally travel beyond an invisible, inviolable boundary:

> In the lessened pressure of . . . upper waters the gas enclosed within the air
> bladder expands. The fish becomes lighter and more buoyant. Perhaps he tries
> to fight his way down again, opposing the upward lift with all the powers of
> his muscles. If he does not succeed, he "falls" to the surface, injured and
> dying, for the abrupt release of pressure from without causes distention and
> rupture of tissues. (Carson 1951: 49)

The image of a fish falling upwards is a disorienting reversal and the shift
from a general "they" to a particular "he" is more direct. Carson includes all
fishes initially, but then assigns male sex to the fish that falls, thereby direct-
ing her address to those in human societies who identify with the correspond-
ing gender. Carson's description shows that even in a system made for fish,
predators can go too far and consequences for transgression are steep. Here,
the implication is that privilege accorded in human society is neither constant
nor complete.

Ecofeminist literary critic Josephine Donovan (1998) explains that strategies that encourage identification with the "other" nudge readers toward an
important awakening. For Donovan, it is "not a matter of making the dominated sensitive to the realities of the dominator, which she generally knows
all too well," because "most humans, even those who are themselves dominated because of gender or race, are dominators/exploiters of animals and
other natural entities" (Donovan 1998: 92–93). Confronting readers with
borders reminds them, particularly those who enjoy greater access to social,
economic, and political power, that "they/I do not know, cannot have, everything" (Friedman 1998: 53). Carson uses shifts between subject positions to

invite readers to reconstitute the "other" as a subject and sensitize "domina-
tors to the realities of the dominated" (Donovan 1998: 92). This shift from
general to particular encourages readers with greater proximity to the privileges accorded white, heterosexual men in Western society to relate to the
"other" as a subject occupying a different location in the same system, without the shame and guilt that hinders examinations of personal privilege.

Carson's centering of marginal environments and privileging of characteristics associated with marginal existence are revealed most clearly in her
proposition that the marginal world of the coast has not always been on the
margin. In fact, while Carson contends that the ocean is the mother of all
things that do and have lived, she locates the site where life began as the
marginal world of the shore. Carson explains that it is the shore "where the
drama of life played its first scene on earth and perhaps even its prelude" and
it is the shore "where the forces of evolution are at work today, as they have
been since the appearance of what we know as life" (Carson 1955: 7). She
reinforces this idea in *The Sea Around Us* by arguing that,

> [f]ar from being the original home of life, the deep sea has probably been
> inhabited for a relatively short time. While life was developing and flourishing
> in the surface waters, along the shores, and perhaps in the rivers and swamps,
> two immense regions of the earth still forbade invasion by living things. These
> were the continents and the abyss. (Carson 1951: 54)

In this passage, Carson dislocates the center of land (the continents) and the
center of the sea (the abyss) by focusing her discussion of the origin of life on
the borders between land and sea. In a comment that invokes Gayatri Spivak,
Trinh T. Minh-Ha (1991: 17) declares that from the perspective of "others,"
the "center itself is marginal" and that a "woman narrates a displacement as
she relentlessly shuttles between the center and the margin." Carson embraces such displacement by sharing narratives of beings that prosper in
shifting, marginal landscapes.

According to Carson, life in marginal worlds requires resiliency, flexibil-
ity, adaptability, and a great tolerance for ambiguity. She explains that each
creature that lives on or passes through the shore, "by the very fact of its
existence there, gives evidence that it has dealt successfully with the realities
of its world" (Carson 1955: 11). She highlights the qualities that are essential
for survival and explains that,

> [b]y marvelous adaptations of form and structure, the inhabitants of the world
> between the tide lines are enabled to live in a zone where the danger of being
> dried up is matched against the danger of being washed away, where for every
> enemy that comes by sea there is another that comes by land, and where the
> most delicate of living tissues must somehow withstand the assault of storm

waves that have power to shift tons of rock or to crack the hardest granite.
(Carson 1951: 159–60)

In her persistent, recurrent return to marginal landscapes, and her steady, consistent exultation of life on the border, Carson demonstrates "a working out of and an appeal to another sensibility, another consciousness of the condition of marginality: that in which marginality is the condition of the center" (Trinh 1991: 18). By centering the marginal perspective, Carson validates the experience of readers who may not be accustomed to such accommodation. This alone is powerfully transformative. For enfranchised readers, Carson promotes empathy and challenges the "naturalness" of social order based on difference.

For readers who are unfamiliar with the experience of living on the margins, or who shuttle between fewer rather than more informing identities, Carson offers additional evidence of the efficacy of border life. She acknowledges that border zones such as "the strips between tropical tide lines" make conditions "difficult for nearly all forms of life" (Carson 1955: 211), yet these areas are frequently heavily populated. There are "cities of mole crabs" on beaches with breaking waves (Carson 1955: 153), and rocks along a turbulent inlet are "matted with creatures that love the swiftly moving current and the ceaseless eddy" (Carson 1941: 141–42). Carson celebrates life that flourishes in places that seem dangerously frenetic. For example, she notes that,

> wherever two currents meet, especially if they differ sharply in temperature or salinity, there are zones of great turbulence and unrest, with water sinking or rising up from the depths and with shifting eddies and foam lines at the surface. At such places the richness and abundance of marine life reveals itself most strikingly. (Carson 1951: 23)

Reminiscent of the border culture that produced Anzaldúa's mestiza, Carson's affirmation of vibrant communities emerging from chaos remains both relevant and potent. Melissa Wright (2000: 209) revisits *Borderlands/La Frontera* and revises Anzaldúa's image of the mestiza in order to reflect the evolution of border culture at the turn of the twenty-first century. She proposes that by "reimagining the border not as [a] place of division but as [a] unified seam, where different manifestations of an essentially unified culture meet" the mestiza of present time "foresees an emerging geography that will ground a reinvigorated cultural and feminist politics." In her description of borders and border life in the natural world at mid-twentieth century, Carson anticipates border studies developed during the late twentieth century by Anzaldúa, Wright, and others. In a split with Anzaldúa, Carson tends to prefer ambiguity over hybridity to describe the most radical subjects in the borderlands.

In the sea books, Carson regularly brings to the fore indeterminate and transitional beings. Often, these observations are contained within discussions of evolution as when she notes "a small snail whose race is moving landward" (Carson 1955: 244) and remarks that "snails that are now terrestrial came of marine ancestry, their forebears having at some time made the transitional crossing of the shore" (Carson 1955: 50). Imposing additional complexity, Carson claims that the first living things were "mysterious borderline forms that were not quite plants, not quite animals, barely over the intangible line that separates the non-living from the living" (Carson 1951: 7). On present-day coastlines, Carson finds examples of beings caught clearly, if not neatly between worlds. Ghost crabs seem "almost a land animal," but they must carry sea water in their branchial chambers in order to breathe (Carson 1955: 157). There is a species of large white crab living in the Bahamas and southern Florida that is undertaking the transition from sea to land life; the adult form breathes air and lives on land, but the early stages of its life cycle are completed in the sea (Carson 1955: 245). Carson reports that the emergence of land forms began some 350 million years ago during Silurian time, and that the first creature to cross the threshold was an arthropod:

> It must have been something like a modern scorpion, but, unlike some of its descendents, it never wholly severed the ties that united it to the sea. It lived a strange life, half-terrestrial, half-aquatic, something like that of the ghost crabs that speed along the beaches today, now and then dashing into the surf to moisten their gills. (Carson 1951: 12)

On essentially the same shores, successive generations of "pioneering mollusks and crustaceans are learning to live out of the sea from which they recently came" (Carson 1955: 244). With example after example of intermediate or transitional life forms, Carson encourages an acceptance of fluidity in identity at the same time she introduces *process* as an appealing alternative to progress.

For Friedman, the "future of feminism and other progressive movements lies . . . in a turning outward, an embrace of contradiction, dislocation, and change" (Friedman 1998: 4). For ecofeminists such as Donovan, turning outward must include a deliberate process of locating subjects outside of the self and a conscientious effort to resist the pressure to objectify others, whether human or nonhuman. Donovan describes the concept of "attentive love," identified by Simone Weil and advanced by Iris Murdoch, as "a central theoretical component of the contemporary feminist ethic of care" (Donovan 1998: 88). Carson demonstrates a kind of attentive love for readers by actively seeking subjects in the natural world, by looking beyond what she sees, and sometimes, by not looking at all.

While Carson gathers important information from passive observation, she nevertheless reminds readers throughout the sea books that searching for subjects is an active and purposeful pursuit. Some of the "most beautiful pools of the shore are not exposed to the view of the casual passer-by. They must be searched for" instead (Carson 1955: 117). Searching for subjects may require a change in expectations as well as perspective. For example, Carson explains that in some areas, "signs of living creatures are often visible, if not the animals themselves" (Carson 1955: 131). Introducing the chapter "The Rocky Shores," she states that at high tide, when the brimming fullness of the sea advances on the bayberrys and junipers lining the coast,

> one can easily suppose that nothing at all lived in or on or under these waters of the sea's edge. For nothing is visible . . . all the creatures of the tidal rocks are hidden from view, but the gulls know what is there, and they know that in time the water will fall away again and give them entrance to the strip between the tide lines. (Carson 1955: 39)

While much is hidden from human eyes, it is not hidden to all; however, the gulls' way of knowing is superior to humans not because their sight is better, but because they know when, where, and how to look. For ecofeminists, unseating vision, or "mind" knowledge, "from a privileged position as a way of knowing, or positing the notions that "bodies know" are powerful strategies to destabilize attitudes that promote objectification and exploitation of other humans as well as nonhuman nature (Legler 1997: 230). In addition to encouraging readers to look actively for subjects, Carson promotes strategies that engage senses associated with body knowledge to compensate for the limitations of I/eye-sight.

For humans, the capacity to see and consequently describe only one thing at a time reinforces a consciousness of alienation, of separation from nature. Carson reminds readers that sight can deceive and even prohibit access to, and understanding of, complex systems. For Carson, seeking subjects includes actively compensating for the limitations and imperfections of human vision. Sometimes, this is accomplished by simply drawing attention to optical illusions such as when sea foam connects grass stalks in a sandy marsh so completely that it looks "like a beach thickly grown with short grass" when, in reality, the grass stands a foot tall with two-thirds its height submerged beneath the water and froth (Carson 1941: 83). Frequently, Carson adjusts for limitations in human perception as when she points out that "the most obvious patterning of the surface waters is indicated by color" to human senses, although these colors are only indirect signs of the presence or absence of conditions needed to support life; it may be other factors, "invisible to the eye, [that] determine where marine creatures may live" (Carson 1951:

20–21). In the following example, Carson models the process by which humans might begin to see beyond the range of sight. She explains:

> Somewhere in the crystal clarity of the pool my eye—or so it seemed—could detect a fine mist of infinitely small particles, like dust motes in a ray of sunshine. Then as I looked more closely the motes had disappeared and there seemed to be once more only that perfect clarity, and the sense that there had been an optical illusion. Yet I knew it was only the human imperfection of my vision that prevented me from seeing those microscopic hordes that were the prey of the groping, searching tentacles [of the resident hydroids] I could barely see. (Carson 1955: 116–17)

Accommodating limitations of human eyesight is an acknowledgment of the limitations of the subject-observer. Compensating requires active involvement on the part of the seer, and this consciousness can distract the observer from imposing his or her experience onto the observed thereby interrupting the process by which the subject viewed becomes an object. Finally, upsetting the correspondence between vision and knowledge disrupts the binary system that undergirds Western cultural logic. Carson makes the connection between vision and knowledge clear when she notes that eels passing from inland marshes to rivers and through the surf to the sea then pass "from human sight and almost from human knowledge" (Carson 1941: 229). Multiple senses and mindful intent are necessary to fill the gaps left vacant by the limitations of what the I/eye knows.

In her study *Off the Reservation: Reflections of Boundary-Busting, Border-Crossing Loose Canons*, Paula Gunn Allen (1998) asserts that stories about landscapes can reveal important insights into human identity. She proposes that the "smells, sounds, and tactile sensations that go with a locale are as central to its human significance as the sights" and that it is within stories that "all the dimensions of human sensation, perception, conception, and experience" are able to come together in meaningful ways (Allen 1998: 234). In addition to attending to the limitations of vision, Carson further confounds reliance on sight by featuring every sensation capable of stimulating body knowledge in her descriptions of the natural world. A sand dollar is "soft as felt" (Carson 1955: 139) and Irish moss has the texture of Turkish toweling (Carson 1955: 80). Appealing to the metaphysical, Carson recalls her first meeting with an ocean current. She was overwhelmed by the "sense of a powerful presence felt but not seen, its nearness made manifest but never revealed" (Carson 1951: 131–32). Displacing vision with other senses in the pursuit of subjects has an additional benefit. Body knowledge creates its own dialectic whereby readers discover hidden aspects of themselves, as they learn to relate to the perspective of the "other."

When Carson listens to the natural world, she emphasizes how sound can connect us to each other, whether human to human, or human to nonhuman nature. She reminds us that it is never quiet, never still at the edge of the sea. Along the rocky coast, it is clear how deeply Carson relates to the landscape as a subject when she finds "few obvious signs of life to break the spell of brooding isolation" except for "little murmurings and whisperings born of the movements of air and water" over the jagged rocks; sounds she calls audible voices of a nonhuman, intertidal world (Carson 1955: 207). Some passages are exquisite, showcasing the beauty of sounds through alliteration, cadence, and other poetic devices. On a quiet night, the sound of breakers on a barrier beach are "but the distant voice of the sea" and, hushed almost to a sigh, there reports "a sort of rhythmic exhalation as though the sea, too, were asleep outside the gates of sound" (Carson 1941: 14).

Carson uses highly evocative language again when she plays with the correspondence between silence and sound during her regular walk through the woods to the sea. She describes bearded lichen hanging in delicate bunches from branches overhead. A supple expanse of reindeer moss carpets the forest floor beneath her feet. Despite the loveliness of the wood, it is the oscillation between silence and sound that moves her most. She recalls,

> [I]n the quiet of that place even the voice of the surf is reduced to a whispered echo and the sounds of the forest are but the ghosts of sound—the faint sighing of evergreen needles in the moving air; the creaks and heavier groans of half-fallen trees resting against their neighbors and rubbing bark against bark; the light rattling fall of a dead branch broken under the feet of a squirrel and sent bounding and ricocheting earthward. (Carson 1955: 41)

Carson establishes a mood that is both interior and intimate with the sense that she is moving through a room filled with others. The sighs and whispers overheard suggest communication, not just utterance. The scene is inclusive and demonstrates integration on every level. The living, the dead, and the elemental form a community through which Carson—and apparently a squirrel—passes. Finally, Carson's voice is deliberate as she models interaction with the natural world based on listening and hearing.

Searching always for the subject/self in the "other," for Donovan, results in a "meditative attentiveness," a process that is critical and creative, requiring both "great patience and the disciplined ability to resist imposing ones' own signifying text upon the other"; the result is pronounced, because it allows "to come into being entities which would otherwise remain concealed" (Donovan 1998: 88, 92). Additionally, Carson demonstrates what Legler refers to as "an ethic of caring friendship, or 'a loving eye,' as a principle for relationships with nature" (Legler 1997: 230). When returning a medium-size man-of-war she'd found stranded on a South Carolina beach to the sea, Carson shares a radical discovery with readers. While some in the family of siphonophores can deflate air sacs in order to sink below turbulent waters, a Portuguese man-of-war cannot. After wading out into chilly March seas to release the creature, Carson watches it negotiate the waves and the ebbing tide:

> Sometimes with my help, sometimes without, it would manage to take off again, visibly adjusting the shape and position of the sail as it scudded along before the wind. . . . But whether in difficulty or enjoying momentary success, there was nothing passive in the attitude of the creature. There was, instead, a strong illusion of sentience. This was no helpless bit of flotsam, but a living creature exerting every means at its disposal to control its fate. (Carson 1955: 172–73)

Carson begins with thoughtful attention and a caring attitude. She observes agency, but is unwilling to personify the man-of-war by determining its affect. She recognizes a will to live which she accepts as like consciousness. Significantly, it is not the will to live which she identifies, but the man-of-war's drive to control its fate.

In another revealing moment, Carson recounts impressions of a live West Indian basket star. She remembers the "searching, exploring, testing branchlets at the tips of the arms" and remarks that they remind her of the "delicate tendrils by which a growing vine seeks out places to which it may attach itself" (Carson 1955: 225). She explains to readers that this is a rare scientific opportunity; however, she describes the encounter as if meeting a friend. She recognizes the basket star's "extraordinary and somehow fragile beauty" (Carson 1955: 225). She responds to its vulnerability with ethical authority when she relates, "I had no wish to 'collect' it; to disturb such a being would have seemed a desecration" (Carson 1955: 225). For Donovan, if we are to adjust human interaction with the natural world, we must encourage the "development of forms of attention that enhance awareness of the living environment, that foster respect for its reality as a separate, different, but knowable entity" (Donovan 1998: 92). Clearly, when Carson encountered the natural world, it was with the expectation that she would meet subjects, and the strategies that she advances in the sea books are heuristic devices that offer the potential for emancipatory awakening. It is this potential that makes Carson's early work at least as radical as *Silent Spring*; regrettably, the sea books have received only a fraction of the attention they deserve.

NOTES

1. *Under the Sea-Wind* was originally published in November 1941, just one month prior to the attack on Pearl Harbor. Only two thousand copies were sold (Lear 1997: 105).

2. For examples of critical perspectives on Carson, see Marcia Myers Bonta's (1991) *Women in the Field: America's Pioneering Women Naturalists*, Vera Norwood's (1993) *Made from this Earth: American Women and Nature*, Rebecca Raglon's (1997) "Rachel Carson and Her Legacy," Henrietta Nickels Shirk's (1997) "Technical Writer as EcoWriter: The Rhetorical Legacy of Rachel Carson," and Craig Waddell's (2000) *And No Birds Sing: Rhetorical Analy-*

ses of Rachel Carson's Silent Spring. H. Patricia Hynes' (1989) *The Recurring Silent Spring* is an excellent assessment of Carson's science and offers suggestions for identifying the radical components of Carson's literary legacy. These works and the majority of scholarship on Carson's work focus nearly exclusively on *Silent Spring*.

3. As a woman scientist during the first part of the twentieth century, Carson's world was circumscribed by social restrictions and diminished expectations which have been chronicled by a number of excellent biographers, the most thorough and comprehensive being Linda Lear's (1997) *Rachel Carson: Witness for Nature*. Additional scholarship on the history of women in science include Marina Benjamin's (1993) *A Question of Identity: Women, Science, and Literature*, and Nancy Tuana's (1989) *Feminism and Science*. Margaret W. Rossiter's (1995) *Women Scientists in America: Before Affirmative Action, 1940-1972* provides important context for understanding Carson's tenuous situation as sole breadwinner for an extended family during a time when women were increasingly driven out of the professions in both public and private sectors.

Chapter Five

Decadent Desire

The Dream of Disembodiment in J. K. Huysmans' A Rebours

Monique M. LaRocque

Most critics of the late nineteenth-century Decadent period have examined it in opposition to the Romantic and Realist literary tradition before it, and in opposition to late nineteenth-century bourgeois culture. Decadent writers were weary of the Realists' aesthetics grounded in everyday reality and, at the same time, rejected the Romantic exaltation of nature as both a panacea to societal ills (stemming from urban industrialization) and as a site of spiritual comfort. According to the French novelist J. K. Huysmans, Naturalist writers in the latter part of the century had exhausted their repertoire of themes, and the formulaic and reductive quality of their plots was stifling to creativity. Art, he believed, should not be reduced to reproducing everyday reality. Huysmans, and the Decadent writers who followed him, attempted "to diverge as far as possible from nature, in an overt repudiation of the classical dogma that the aim of all art [was] the imitation of nature" (Pierrot 1981: 166).

Most troubling to the Decadent imagination was the idea that humans were enslaved to the needs of their physical bodies and were at the mercy of a seemingly indifferent and mechanistic Nature that subjected man to its laws of heredity and evolution. Nature seemed repetitive and banal, no longer providing inspiration or mystery. They turned instead toward man-made artifice for their source of artistic inspiration and consolation. The Decadent aesthete rejected nature and attempted to separate himself as much as possible from his natural surroundings, as well as from those aspects of himself that most reminded him of his animal-like nature, for example, his body,

sexuality, and by extension, women. In attempting to circumscribe his hu-
manness, and thus his superiority over nature, he negotiated his identity as an
aesthetic body, seeking to separate himself from all he believed incapable of
rising above their nature. Women were considered to be incapable of valuing
true art and were thought to lack aesthetic appreciation and sensibility; thus
they were regarded as a lower order of humanity and less developed mentally
and spiritually than men. This understanding of women as lacking an aesthetic sensibility reinforced an ideological view already well-established in the
Western mind: women were closer to nature than men, who were closer to
culture. Women were thought to be incapable of achieving an intellectual, if
not spiritual, transcendence over nature, and were bound to an insipid material reality. As reproductive bodies, they were an incessant reminder of man's
place in the natural world and his embeddedness in life. Thus, in their rejection of organic life, and their desire to flee the mediocrity of bourgeois
culture, the Decadents sought escape into an aesthetic world that excluded
women. Adopting a Platonic view that only (certain) men had the ability to
recognize material reality as an inferior manifestation of a greater, transcendent reality, the Decadents held aesthetics to be their exclusive and privileged domain.

The literature of the late nineteenth-century Decadent period is fraught
with anti-women and anti-nature sentiments. Although there is much scholarship critiquing the Decadents' misogyny and anti-nature attitudes, there is no
sustained study of the overt alignment of women and nature as realms separate from and inferior to the (assumed) superior realms of man and culture. I
will argue that the Decadents' love of artifice and patriarchal negation of
women is consistent with a capitalist bourgeois agenda that seeks independence from both women and nature.

My reading of the Decadent period is largely informed by ecological and
feminist literary criticism, and most specifically, ecofeminism—a theoretical
discourse that explores the link between the oppression of women and the
domination of nature. In general, ecofeminists critique hierarchical dualisms
which have a long-standing tradition in Western thought and are conceptually structured by a mind/body division. Particularly useful to a critique of the
Decadent period is ecofeminist Val Plumwood's theory that Western dualisms are characterized by a logical structure of otherness and negation, where
the undesirable *other* is made inferior and is subjugated. "A dualism," Plumwood states in *Feminism and the Mastery of Nature*, "results from a certain
kind of denied dependency on a subordinated other. This relationship of
denied dependency determines a certain kind of logical structure, in which
the denial and the relation of domination/subordination shape the identity of
both the relata" (1993: 41). Gender gets inscribed on Western dualistic thinking so that the feminine embodies those characteristics deemed least desirable by the rational, objective, masculine viewpoint. This mapping of gender

onto the nature/culture dualism establishes a definitive hierarchy between the deemed superior realm of masculine culture/artifice/inorganic and the deemed inferior realm of feminine nature/natural/organic. An ecofeminist perspective is especially useful because it invites us to view Decadence in its broad, historical, and cultural context and enables us to ascertain the dualistic tensions and ideological features it shares with its bourgeois contemporaries. Although Decadent writers outwardly reject bourgeois values, they embrace certain notions about the inferior status of women and nature in relationship to *man*kind that are fundamental to bourgeois ideology. Thus, while most critics have argued that literary Decadence was hostile to bourgeois values and undermined the development of a capitalist society, this study shows that the Decadents' love of artifice and desire to transcend their biological/natural condition were consistent with a modern bourgeois, capitalist ideology.

In this chapter, I bring an ecofeminist perspective to the study of the quintessential nineteenth-century Decadent work: J. K. Huysmans' *A Rebours* (*Against the Grain*). Des Esseintes, the decadent hero *par excellence*, seeks to create a world for himself that is artfully superficial and completely independent of women and nature. His predilection for artificial, virtual realities aligns him with his bourgeois contemporaries who also seek to replace nature with artifice, and who ultimately imagine human freedom to be independent from nature and natural processes. Attention to the logic of dualisms that are operative in the novel is particularly useful in understanding the paradox of Des Esseintes' position regarding women and nature, and women and bourgeois culture. Des Esseintes not only rejects women and nature as inferior but also rejects bourgeois society as inferior, thereby embracing and enacting a structural logic of domination and negation consistent with the Western dualistic tradition. There is a distinctive master/slave logic operative in *A Rebours*. Des Esseintes sees himself occupying the superior position in his male, artificial, rational, high-art space, and rejects the undesirable— female, natural, irrational, low art, and bourgeois—*other*, ascribing to it a feminine ethos. That is, he appropriates the master identity through multiple exclusions of inferior and subordinate others. Andreas Huyssen, in *After the Great Divide*, has argued that the gendering of mass culture as feminine and inferior is historically specific to the late nineteenth century. "It is indeed striking to observe," he notes, "how the political, psychological, and aesthetic discourse around the turn of the century consistently and obsessively genders mass culture and the masses as feminine, while high culture, whether traditional or modern, clearly remains the privileged domain of male activities" (1986: 47). This gendering of mass culture as feminine repeats a common theme in patriarchal culture whereby the undesirable other is always relegated to an inferior status.

In this novel of little plot and action, Des Esseintes, the aesthete and antihero, escapes to a country retreat at Fontenay where he quarantines himself in a completely artificial environment, sealed off from all reminders of the natural world and intent to transcend his own biological nature. We first learn of Des Esseintes' "rejection" of nature in favor of artifice and his intended aesthetic project when, in chapter 2, he states that "Nature has had her day" and "the time is undoubtedly come when her productions must be superseded by art" (*AR* 22). This announcement emerges from a discussion wherein Des Esseintes is pondering the merits of *illusion* and the superiority of the imagination over the vulgar reality of the material world. Des Esseintes thinks, for example, that "by just salting your bath and mixing with the water . . . a compound of sulphate of soda, hydrochlorate of magnesia and lime . . . the illusion is undeniable . . . you are as good as at the seaside" (21). Here he celebrates the potential of artifice to recreate the real experience without the material inconveniences (in this case, having to travel all the way to the seaside). He hopes to live inside the world of books, the world of illusion, the aesthetic life of the mind, without any dependence on anything reminiscent of the outside world.

It is important to note that his ambition to completely separate from nature reveals an underlying assumption that it is not only desirable but also *possible* to be separated from the natural world. This assumption was not an aberration of the Decadent imagination. By the end of the nineteenth century, the idea of nature as a sphere outside of human culture was already firmly established in the Western mind. A look at the changing urban landscape of Paris from the early part of the nineteenth century to Haussmann's massive re-constructive transformations of this landscape in the 1860s suggests the potential for an important psychic shift in peoples' relationship to nature. City dwellers were encouraged to think of nature as something distant from their immediate living environment. The natural landscape was being destroyed to accommodate the expanding city limits and those natural spaces that were left intact factored into a larger conceptual metropolitan design. Paris, which retained a medieval character even as late as the 1820s, was soon to be transformed into a highly structured and gridded metropolis with all physical spaces, including natural ones, organized according to a rational plan. As Nicholas Green argues in *The Spectacle of Nature*, gardens like the Bois de Boulogne, Vincennes, and the Buttes Chaumont were laid out to "*re*-present nature" (1990: 69). The material conditions were ripe at this time for a new and distinctive appropriation of nature as a consumer commodity in the new market economy. Natural spaces were seen as an outside *other* and mostly as products to be consumed for leisure and pleasure in the form of tourism, as sites of entertainment, or as visual spectacles.

The idea of nature was a socially and ideologically determined construct, produced and circulated within the larger historical structures of a material and capitalist ideology. Huysmans appropriates this particular metropolitan conception of nature; Des Esseintes, himself a product of Paris, regards nature as a separate realm, something to be enjoyed as a picture. On the day that he searches for the cottage that will be his retreat, he gazes down on the village and its surroundings and reflects on the landscape as a *representation* rather than as a living environment itself:

> As for the village itself, he had hardly seen it. Only at night, from his window, he had looked out over the silent landscape that stretches down to the foot of a hill on the summit of which rise the batteries of the Bois de Verrieres.
>
> In the shadow, to right and left, loomed other dimly seen masses, terracing the hillside and dominated by other far-off batteries and fortifications, the high revetments of which seemed in the moonlight as if washed in with silver pigment upon a dark background of sky.
>
> The plain lay partly in the shadows cast by the hills, while the centre, where the moonlight fell, looked as if it were powdered with starch and smeared with cold-cream; in the warm air that fanned the pale grass and brought with it a spicy perfume, the trees stood out clearly silhouetted with their shaggy leaves and thin stems, which threw black bars of shadow across the chalky earth strewed with pebbles that sparkled like shards of broken crockery.
>
> The artificial, rather theatrical air of this landscape was to Des Esseintes's taste. (*AR* 23–24)

Des Esseintes makes of this natural landscape a picture, or painted canvas, neatly framed from his window. The batteries seem brushed with silver pigment onto the dark background of the canvas. The picture also borrows some man-made elements, such as cold cream and shards of broken crockery, which add to the artificiality of the scene. This perspective gives rise to a sense of detachment and spectatorship, a perspective that Des Esseintes shares with his metropolitan bourgeois contemporaries. Like them, he imagines improving upon nature—a recurring motif throughout *A Rebours*. The subject/object distance allows for the possibility of manipulation—adding to the picture (i.e., cold cream, broken crockery) what is deemed necessary to improve and complete the scene. Des Esseintes is an observer, not a participant in this environment. Because he perceives it as artificial and removed, he has no attachment to it. This attitude of indifference facilitates the potential for exploiting nature and is an attitude shared by his bourgeois contemporaries in the increasingly industrialized world. From an ecocritical perspective, this insistence on the artificiality of the real exposes the perverse relationship between humans and nature—a relationship that denies dependence on the very environment that is necessary to sustain life.

Des Esseintes' infamous turtle most outrageously exemplifies the perversity of commodifying nature. When Des Esseintes purchases a turtle and tries to make an artwork of it, the turtle is unable to sustain its role as an aesthetic object. Desiring *something* that will bring out the various tones of his Oriental carpet, Des Esseintes strolls through the Parisian streets, window shop-

ping—like the other bourgeois shoppers—for his desired object. Des Esseintes purchases the turtle to furnish his home, just as he would purchase
any other commodity on the luxury goods market. He then tries to *improve*
the turtle (i.e., nature) by having its shell inlaid with gold and carefully
selected precious stones. He turns the turtle loose on his carpet, only to
discover, several days later, that the turtle is dead, having been unable to
carry the burden of the artificial load. Indeed, the hyperbole of this episode
suggests that Huysmans is mocking Des Esseintes. The desire to place the
turtle in a foreign environment and make of it a piece of artwork seems
perverse to say the least. However, an ecocritical perspective would suggest
that the turtle that Des Esseintes purchases *has already been* perverted and
made into art by being extracted from its natural habitat and placed in the
unnatural environment of the shopkeepers' tank. In the tank, the turtle is an
aesthetic object framed by the glass of the tank, and is displayed as an object
for consumption. Des Esseintes, in other words, treats the turtle no differently or no less reverently than does the petty bourgeois shopkeeper. His act
merely exposes, in a more outrageous fashion, the commodification of the
turtle. The turtle, like the tiger skins and blue-foxes' pelts he has scattered
about his Fontenay cottage, is no more, nor less, than a commodity. Des
Esseintes only takes to another level the perversity of bourgeois capitalist
values, which seek to dominate and control all living creatures and exploit
them for mercenary ends. By exaggerating Des Esseintes' pose, Huysmans'
text exposes the hypocrisy and ultimate pathology of the bourgeois' disinte-
grating relationship with the natural environment.

Des Esseintes' desire to seek refuge from the city and his subsequent
purchase of a country cottage are consistent with a larger sociocultural tendency, and should therefore not be interpreted as his unique psychopatholog-
ical act. The acquisition of a residence in the countryside was similarly
desired and sought by those bourgeois who could afford the luxury. Green
suggests that the purchase of these country homes was one important aspect
of consuming nature as a panacea for urban environmental problems; it also
signified a superior social status for the buyer as he was able to distinguish
himself as a man of wealth. These country homes promised a safe haven
away from the frenzy of the city and an intimate private world where one
could go about one's business unseen. But as Green also states, "The privacy
of nature meant being invisible to others, your own powers to *see* were
paramount. The house as eye on to the countryside was constantly reiterat-
ed. . . . The language of views and panoramas prescribed a certain visual
structure to the *nature* experience. . . . Environmental values were here
articulated in relation to visual modes of consumption that enabled the visitor
simultaneously to look at 'the picture' and plunge into sensation" (1990:
87–88). Des Esseintes' own cottage is remote and isolated, significantly
located at the top of a hill that overlooks the village and surrounding country-

side. He experiences a sense of godlike empowerment and mastery from being able to look without being seen. He chooses the night and the artificial light of lamps over the natural light of the sun. He sleeps away the days so that he is awake and master of his domain at night "holding that then a man [is] more truly at home, more himself and his own master . . . moreover, he reap[s] a special and peculiar satisfaction from finding himself in a room brilliantly lighted up, the only place alive and awake among surrounding houses all buried in sleep and darkness" (*AR* 12). Therefore, while Des Esseintes will certainly carry artificiality to its extreme by isolating himself completely within an artificially constructed abode and secluding himself entirely from other people, he does not act fundamentally different than his bourgeois counterparts, who also live increasingly within artificial, or constructed landscapes, and who aspire to ultimate individualism.

The Decadents' abhorrence of the bourgeoisie is partly due to its attempt to emulate the aristocracy and attain the same material wealth and advantages of the nobility. If the bourgeois can live as the aristocrat, then the aristocracy loses its significance as a class of privilege. Des Esseintes' particular form of neurotic disconnectedness from others is intensified by the urban industrial environment, and the subsequent disruption of social hierarchies; indeed, his social status as well as personal identity are threatened with erasure. As part of the dying aristocracy, his class has lost its function and status in the newly established utilitarian world; his inherited fortune obviates his need to work, while his class no longer controls the political environment or the cultural and social scene. Des Esseintes, as the quintessential dandy, cannot be easily classified in the new economy, belonging to neither the masculine public domain of production (he doesn't need or desire to work), nor the feminine, private domain of consumption (he is not female).

It is important to note that the bourgeois associated the Decadent dandy with femininity because of his precarious status in the industrial, utilitarian world, his propensity for shopping and leisure, and his lavish adornment of the body. However, the end-of-the-century aesthete himself appropriates the feminine only insofar as to signal his difference from the bourgeois male producer, on the one hand, and his difference from the bourgeois female consumer, on the other. "If the aesthete and dandy shares with women an identity as consumer," Rita Felski argues in *The Counterdiscourse of the Feminine*, "it becomes imperative for him to signal the superior taste and the qualitative difference of his own aesthetic response" (1991: 1100). So while Des Esseintes adopts the consumer pose to the nth degree—a pose he disdains when paraded by bourgeois women—he still claims the superiority of his own tastes which are identified with high art, as opposed to the sentimental kitsch aesthetics identified with women. Similarly while the traits of femininity appropriated by the male aesthete serve to elevate him (in his own mind) above the male bourgeois world, feminine qualities in a woman only confirm her inability to transcend her natural condition (1099). In Decadent literature, women come to embody *all* that is least desirable: nature *and* mass culture. As Felski argues, "Women stand for the most despised aspects of both culture and nature, exemplifying the crass vulgarity and emptiness of modern bourgeois society (woman as archetypal consumer) as well as a natural sentimentality coded as specific to women, an inclination to outpourings of uncontrolled feeling that threaten the disengaged stance of the male aesthete" (1100).

The negation and rejection of the undesirable other is made manifest in *A Rebours*, where women embody the image of mass-produced items that the Decadents deplore. Des Esseintes thinks that women, like mass-produced objects, are all the same; they are unoriginal and uncreative. During one of his walks down memory lane, he reflects on the many beer halls of the Quartier Latin that he once frequented. He recalls peering through the windows of each store (like a window shopper): "Through the half open doors and the windows only partially obscured by coloured panes or curtains he could remember having caught glimpses of women walking up and down with dragging step and out-thrust neck, the way geese waddle" (*AR* 161). These shops stood "one after the other down the side-walk, which they overlook[ed] with a row of signboards all very much alike" (161). The beer halls, like a strip mall of shops lined up one after the other, entice the male passerby to spend his money on the precious commodities within (i.e., women). Here, women are associated with both imbecile animality—geese waddling—and with mass-produced objects of consumption. These beer hall wenches are described as "so many automata wound up at the same time with the same key, uttered in the same tone the same invitations, lavished the same smiles, talked in the same silly phrases indulged in the same absurd reflexions" (162). The reproduction of nature and the mass reproduction of bourgeois industrialism converge. Woman stands in at the nexus of this convergence representing all that is least desirable. She is both nature reproduced over and over again, in the image of geese waddling, and she is bad art, reproduced over and over again, in the form of mechanically reproduced objects. The idea of *reproduction*—both natural procreation and mass production—links both women and nature, on the one hand, and bourgeois technological culture and democracy, on the other. That is, an explicit parallel is made, between women as primary, biological reproductive machines and bourgeois culture. Des Esseintes reacts to women's reproductive ability and downgrades it by comparing women to machines, a concept reminiscent of the Cartesian consideration of the natural world as one great machine.

Des Esseintes' move to Fontenay is a symbolic rejection of the body/women and nature and a move to the world of mind, dream, and imagination. It is precisely his rejection of the body and its reminder of biological dependency that occasions the black dinner party he throws to celebrate his "loss of virility." Interestingly, he recalls this infamous party immediately before withdrawing from society. In this literary tour de force, Des Esseintes serves, on "black-bordered plates," an assortment of black delicacies, such as "Russian black bread . . . game dished up in sauces coloured to resemble liquorice water and boot-blacking," and offers wine in "dark-tinted glasses" (*AR* 11). He also symbolically chokes/kills nature by strewing black coal on the garden walks and pouring ink in the water basin, and replaces ordinary shrubs with cypresses and pines—symbolic trees of death. In this thematic linking of nature (his garden), food, and women (his loss of virility) with the color black, he celebrates the symbolic death of the life-giving. His sexual impotence clearly suggests a link between his loss of carnal desire and his emancipation from the fetters of the real biological/natural world. He even orders that the bedroom he will later inhabit in his retreat be decorated as a Trappist's cell—suggesting his ultimate rejection of women and sexual desire. Des Esseintes' move away from society, then, is his attempt to create a world independent of women and nature by distancing himself from the (sexual) preoccupations of the body; no longer a slave to bodily desire, he is free to retreat to Fontenay where he can attend to the realm of his mind.

In Huysmans' novel, the theme of social degeneration and the diseasing of the body are inseparable from the image of woman who contains that threat. For example, Des Esseintes attributes the downfall of the aristocracy and of his family to both the "progressive effemination of the men" (*AR* 1) and to the vulgar nature of women on whom men have squandered their money, buying "the smiles of women that bewitched and poisoned the descendants of the old families." "Yes," he ponders, "nobility was utterly decayed, dead; aristocracy had fallen into idiocy or filthy pleasures! It was perishing in the degeneracy of its members, whose faculties grew more debased with each succeeding generation till they ended with the instincts of gorillas" (200–201). Des Esseintes envisions women as the culprits of a deteriorating and depraved society. Women entice men into the realm of the flesh, turning even the best of men, the aristocracy, into base and vulgar idiots. This fear of female sexuality and the female body as the basis of a morbidly diseased nature pervades much of late nineteenth-century literature. Although the idea of women luring men to their deaths is an age-old theme in Western literature, it is particularly insistent in the late nineteenth century, as the female body is increasingly associated with disease and social degeneration. In his study of *A Rebours,* Charles Bernheimer notes in *Figures of Ill Repute* that

> it is tempting to limit the significance of the . . . repellent images of female sexuality by ascribing them to the idiosyncrasy of Huysmans's peculiar neurotic sensibility. But they only take to the extreme point of nauseous disgust the obsessive fear of woman's sexual nature, epitomized by the prostitute, that

pervades the male imagination, both novelistic and scientific, throughout the
nineteenth century and that reaches a kind of hysterical paroxysm in its last
two decades. (1997: 247)

The theme of the corrupt and diseased female body is prevalent in Huysmans' text. Des Esseintes' hatred and fear of woman and nature is most
emphatically expressed in a nightmare, which is described, significantly, in
the middle chapter of the novel, suggesting the centrality of the nightmare's
theme to the meaning of the text. In this dream, woman is personified by a
Flower, which itself is represented as Syphilis. Des Esseintes is horrified by
the Flower, as he catches sight of "the savage Nidularium blossom under her
meagre thighs, with its sword blades gaping in blood-red hollows" (*AR* 93).
He must "shut[s] his eyes so as not to see the dreadful eyes of the Syphilis
glaring at him through the wall" (*AR* 93). His fear has as its roots the threat of
castration, a threat that remains consistent throughout the novel. Here, the
vagina dentata, which haunted the dreams of other fin-de-siècle writers
(Showalter 1990:148), provides the castrating image of the deadly female
body—the terrible mouth ready to devour the male viewer. Bernheimer
argues that the fear of the castrated female body functions as the driving
force of Huysmans' creative process, and that this lacking female body is
inextricably connected to a decomposing organic nature. He states that
"[t]his vision of organic fertility gone wild joins Huysmans's vision of ram-
pant organic degeneration: both have their fantasmatic origin in the horror of
castration, both identify female sexuality with the organic basis of nature
itself and view that basis as morbidly diseased" (1997: 248). Organic degeneration is always identified with horrid female sexuality and biological life is
portrayed as a "diseased hemorrhaging" (261).

The obsession with the female sexual body and the desire to contain the
threat of both women and nature is an underlying preoccupation of modern,
capitalist culture. That is, these are not merely manifestations of individual
pathologies on the part of the Decadents but point to a broader, cultural
pathology. In this fear of women and nature as the embodiments of decomposing life lies the desire for a non-organic creativity—a creativity deathless
and pure. In essence, this desire is central to the Decadent project, and is
ultimately the significant link to the bourgeois, capitalist imagination—the
desire to create a world independent of women and nature, a produced world
inhabited by produced selves where creation begins at a point far removed
from biology.

Des Esseintes rejects life processes and revolts against the idea of procreation. Significantly, he loses his own mother at an early age, reinforcing
the desirable absence of the mother, a predominant theme in Decadent literature. Des Esseintes' revolt against life and against motherhood is made explicit as he watches a group of youngsters wrestling, lamenting "what mad-

ness to beget children." He rejects the image of women and children altogether, stating, "in the name of pity, useless procreation should be abolished"
(*AR* 158). Most importantly, he fantasizes revenge against his mother, by
imagining violence toward her during sex with other women (10). Des Esseintes' psychopathology is in a sense a reaction to a loss (of the mother), just
as his contemporaries living in a mechanistic world manifest a socio-patho-
logical response to their own alienation from the natural world. The way to
compensate for that loss is to reject, demean, and control—ultimately to
destroy that which is a reminder of that loss.

Des Esseintes' fantasy to recreate himself from a place that is anti-biolog-
ical and anti-natural manifest his desire to break with the syphilitic organic
cycle and be his own (male) mother. The rejection of the organic for the
inorganic, sterile, and artificial betrays a certain fascination with death itself,
in terms of its opposition to life. Herein lies one of the dualities of the
modern ethos—seeing life and death as dichotomies rather than as continu-
ums.

Ironically, Des Esseintes shows ferocious disdain for the self-made man,
yet this ideal seems to hover in the background of his own desires. He wants
to reinvent himself, much as the self-made man seeks to reinvent himself in
the new urban society. Des Esseintes tries to create himself unnaturally by
separating himself entirely from all that is natural and connected to life
processes. In his desire for separation and isolation lies a politics of radical
individualism. David Weir has noted this motivation in *Decadence and the
Making of Modernism*, stating that, "[o]n the one hand, Des Esseintes's removal to Fontenay might be construed as an elitist, aristocratic rejection of
democratic society; on the other hand, the removal is motivated by a desire
for radical self-reliance and the expression of intense individualism" (1995:
93). Des Esseintes' expression of intense individualism participates in a larger social ideology that places tremendous value on the autonomy and self-
reliance of the individual. Ian Watt has observed that industrial capitalism is
one of the most important historical causes for the emergence of this ideology, which probably began to affect society as a whole in the nineteenth
century (1957: 61). Ecopsychologist Sarah Conn sees radical individualism
as a cultural pathology because it overemphasizes the individual psyche and
the needs of the individual while disparaging the notion of community and
interconnectedness. By seeing the individual self as a bounded and masterful
agent, the self merely pursues egoistic aims for the attainment of personal
pleasure and avoidance of personal pain, thereby denying emotional respon-
siveness to others (1995: 162–63). Des Esseintes' inordinate attention to
himself manifests a similar pathology in that he seeks to cut himself off from
all personal relationships and connection to others. He even limits to the
barest necessity his contact with the two servants who attend to him in his
retreat. These domestics pose no threat to his solitude as they are "subdued to

the rigid quietude of cloistered monks, shut off from all communication with the outer world, content to spend their lives in close rooms with doors and windows always shut" (*AR* 17).

The Decadents have been perceived as standing in opposition to bourgeois value, but as this study shows, they are not ultimately challenging the values of the dominant culture. Although Huysmans' text bemoans the degradations of mass culture, it does not offer an alternative paradigm that fundamentally challenges bourgeois, capitalist ideology. On the contrary, Des Esseintes, as the representative decadent hero, embodies a similar Western patriarchal worldview that establishes itself as the superior side in a logic of gendered dualisms. The Decadents function within the same dualistic thinking that separates man from nature, man from woman, mind from body, the artistic elite from middle-class philistinism, and so forth. In the end, it appears that the difference between the Decadents and the bourgeois is a matter of perspective and perhaps degree, but not of fundamental value. Both praise artifice over nature. Both denigrate nature and women. Both function within death-oriented life, seeking to replace the natural/organic with artificiality.

Chapter Six

"Discourse Excellent Music"

Romantic Rhetoric and Ecofeminism in Mary Shelley's
The Last Man

Vicky L. Adams

Music was Mary Shelley's first inspiration in composing *The Last Man*. In December of 1823, when Shelley wrote in her journal about "the discord of words attuned to bad thoughts," of "the worldly minded," she was likely considering the circumstances surrounding her difficult financial situation and also her controversial personal reputation. At twenty-six, she was well-known to liberal and conservative factions as the daughter of feminist Mary Wollstonecraft and radical writer William Godwin and widow of the unconventional poet Percy Shelley. She had returned from Italy to London a few months previously with her one surviving son to some acclaim, as "the author of *Frankenstein*" and also of the novel *Valperga*. In the journal entry, Shelley compares memories of her life in Italy with her present reality.

In addition to expressing her grief, she is most concerned about her imagination and an inability to envision a new fiction. Yet she writes, "Oh music—thou has filled me, raised me to heaven & given me freedom—I must wed my mind to it . . . I may dream of grand ideas—I may see scenes which may enchant me—I may either think of the past or the future as I would have it—or I will arrange in magnificent procession & gorgeos [*sic*] array some wondrous tale of combinations of man's thoughts & passions" (Shelley 1995: 469–70). *The Last Man* reflects this musical influence, where the sublime and pastoral scene is a backdrop for impending global catastrophe. When the news came in May 1824 that Byron had died in Greece the previous month, it only increased Shelley's undiminished sense of loss. Already at work on the novel, she had expressed empathy in her journal the day before for "the last man," a popular literary theme at the time.

As might be expected, the future revealed to Mary Shelley's imagination is apocalyptic rather than hopeful. From the Miltonic epigraph to the near denouement of Haydn's *The Creation*, *The Last Man* is about paradise lost and recreated. However, that paradise is nearly bereft of its human population. In the novel's final volume, when the last residents decide to leave the almost deserted city of London and Britain for a healthier and more habitable climate, it is nevertheless like the first expulsion from Paradise. The narrator Lionel Verney writes the valediction for the human species' capacities— politics, technology, and the arts. He bids farewell to eloquence, poetry, philosophy, the visual harmony of architecture, sculpture, painting, and theater. He eulogizes, "Farewell to music and the sound of song; to the marriage of instruments, where the concord of soft and harsh unites in sweet harmony" (Shelley 1996: 252).

Near the novel's conclusion, a few weary survivors journey past the awe-inspiring view of the Alps on their way to Geneva, when they suddenly hear something remarkable: "O music, in this our desolation, we had forgotten thee!" Their reverence expresses their wonder of nature as well. Yet they soon recognize the music as a familiar Haydn aria, "New-Created World," following the dramatic moment in the oratorio when the chorus resoundingly proclaims the appearance of light and Chaos subsides.[1] Although seemingly otherworldly, the sound has its source in a village church organ, played by a daughter for her blind, musician father. The "mighty voice" is "inorganic" because it appears to lack a physical origin and is still secondary to the ascendant beauty of nature. The daughter has concealed the depopulation from her father, and the two will also pass away soon. As the plague recedes, nature transmutes into pristine creation for the remnant of humanity (Shelley 1996: 325–26).

The Creation, whose anonymous libretto is based on Genesis 1 and 2, Psalms, and Milton's *Paradise Lost*, had its origins in Haydn's London visit in 1795. The piece was completed in 1798, the year after Mary Shelley was born. Immensely popular throughout Europe, the music was part of "a crucial cultural-historical moment, on the cusp between Enlightenment and Romanticism" (Webster 2005: 151–52). The travelers' arrival at Ferney, where Voltaire once resided, acknowledges this correlation. The libretto moves from God's foundation of the physical universe, to the materialization of plants and animals, and finally the creation of Adam and Eve, accompanied in each instance with angelic praise. While the fall of the rebel angels constitutes the ordering of Chaos, the libretto concludes before the disastrous transgression of Adam and Eve. Thus the couple is depicted in their perfect human embodiment and patriarchal marital happiness. Following their final duet, the angel Uriel warns them that they will remain happy, "If not, misled by false conceit, / Ye strive at more than granted is, / And more desire to know, than know ye should" (Haydn n.d.: pt. 3, no. 32; vi).

In her letter to radical editor (and opera critic) Leigh Hunt around the same time as her December journal entry, Shelley declared, "My great consolation here is music. . . . " Hunt had introduced the Shelleys to his friend Vincent Novello, a prominent musician of Italian descent. She explains that visiting the Novellos' home and attending his chapel concerts had made her an admirer of Haydn. In the letter Shelley modified the text of the oratorio in her appreciation of the first aria: "'A new healed World'—in his *Creation*; what a wonderful stream of sound it is; it puts me in mind of those beautiful lines of Milton 'Untwisting all the chains that tie the hidden soul of harmony'" (Shelley 1980: 408). The quotation is from Milton's Cambridge poem, "L'Allegro," paired with "Il Penseroso." (Handel's choral work *L'Allegro, il Penseroso ed il Moderato* adds a type that correlates with the novel's sets of three main male and female characters. Also, many phrases from Milton's verses could easily be appropriated for fictions about the Byron/Shelley circle.) The two poems are a version of the academic *synkriseis*, in which an orator considers the merits of contrasting propositions—in this case mirth and melancholy (or day and night) (Bradford 2001: 66). Though intended as joyful, the lines Shelley quotes seem also to presage a disruption of individual psychic harmony and the future devastation of the world.

Until recently, *The Last Man* had received a largely negative critical response; yet with a more appreciative appraisal of Mary Shelley's writing and increasing concern about global warming and other serious threats to the biosphere, the novel has become a classic in the canon of environmental literature. The possibility that human-nature interactions cause significant environmental change has only somewhat recently become accepted knowledge. Commencing at the close of the twenty-first century, the narrative examines personal and political responsibility for war and its aftermath. Shelley's novel delineates the conditions that lead from a progressive government and world peace to the near total extinction of the human population—deadly plague and virulent typhus, tremendous winds, earthquakes, storms and floods, and human folly. While *The Last Man* has sources in Enlightenment theories of population decline, it also offers a prescient view of the dangers of climate change and the worldwide impact of transmissible disease.

The identification of Nature as female may lead some readers to presume that the ecological science is outdated or fabricated. Yet Shelley anticipates postmodern science in terms of the Romantic sublime and the personification of Nature. In *Reinventing Eden: The Fate of Nature in Western Culture*, Carolyn Merchant discusses postmodern theories beyond the mechanistic expectation to master nature. Complex adaptive systems include not only ecosystems, but also cultures, nations, and economies (Merchant 2003:

214–15). Recent theories of chaos and complexity dispute one of the fundamental tenets of ecology—the balance of nature. According to Merchant, "Such theories undercut assumptions of a stable, harmonious nature and question holism as a foundation for ecology. They reinforce the idea that predictability, while still useful, is more limited than previously assumed and that nature, while in part a human construct and a representation, is also a real, material, autonomous agent" (2003: 216). Thus "ecocentric personification" integrates rhetoric and ecology as a persuasive trope (Moore 2008: 10).

Merchant cites influential ecologist Daniel Botkin, who considers the metaphor of "discordant harmonies" (*concordia discors*) as a more useful explanation of ecology than the balance of nature. While Merchant emphasizes the need for a "postclassical, postmodern science," this musical image of nature is not a classical ideal but an influential set of ideas about world harmony originating in ancient Greek philosophy. As Botkin states, "This will allow us to find the true idea of a harmony of nature, which as Plotinus wrote so long ago, is by its very essence discordant, created from the simultaneous movements of many tones, the combination of many processes flowing at the same time along various scales, leading not to a simple melody, but to a symphony sometimes harsh and sometimes pleasing" (quoted in Merchant 2003: 216–17). Merchant concludes that the metaphor of discordant harmony and chaos and complexity theories call into question previous egocentric, social-interest, and even ecocentric ethics. She recommends "[a] new ethic of human partnership with nature" in which nature is "an active subject, not a passive object" (Merchant 2003: 217).

EARTHLY PARADISE

At the outset of *The Last Man* the year is 2073, and public opinion has instigated the dissolution of the monarchy and facilitated a successful transition to a reformed government; revolutionary violence has been avoided by the king's compliance to the will of the people. The former king dies soon after and his son Adrian is given the rights to the Earldom of Windsor by the nation, while his haughty widow the ex-queen waits for an opportunity to restore the monarchy. Almost utopian, the cultural background is reminiscent of a Romantic British republican commonwealth in the setting of early modern humanism, nearly contemporary with the emerging science of Bacon and Descartes.[2] Yet even if it occurs far in the future, the abdication of the king creates the potential for either order or disorder. As Carolyn Merchant explains in *The Death of Nature*, "The perception of disorder, so important to the Baconian doctrine of dominion over nature, was also crucial to the rise of mechanism as a rational antidote to the disintegration of the [theory of an] organic cosmos." Descartes' machine became the basic metaphor for the necessary unity of "the cosmos, society, and the self" (Merchant 1989: 192). Although a nonviolent progression toward a more democratic society was a Godwinian political ideal, the narrative reveals the dangerous conjuncture of the vestiges of that cultural inheritance.

Mary Shelley has written the denouement of what Merchant calls the Recovery of Eden story. The goal of finding or restoring a garden paradise has shaped much of Western culture. Since the early modern period, this master narrative has driven Europeans and Euro-Americans in the attempt to domesticate wilderness into a benevolent garden, Westernize indigenous cultures, and transform an unruly female-imaged nature (Merchant 2003: 2). As the novel opens, Verney and his sister Perdita are the forgotten, orphaned offspring of a former friend of the king, embarrassed and impoverished by gambling debts. At the same time that Verney lives a marginal existence as a shepherd, poaching on Adrian's nearby aristocratic holdings, his sister dwells in a country cottage. In *Reinventing Eden*, Merchant describes how the "gamekeeper culture" estates of medieval feudal lords became the protected wilderness areas of a later century (2003: 60–61). As Earl of Windsor, Adrian's patrimony allows him to practice stewardship ethics. Although Verney had considered Adrian to be his class enemy, when he meets him Verney's personal transformation is both immediate and natural. As he describes Adrian, "His vivacity, intelligence, and active spirit of benevolence, completed the conquest. Even at this early age, he was deep read and imbued with the spirit of high philosophy. This spirit gave a tone of irresistible persuasion to his intercourse with others, so that he seemed like an inspired musician, who struck, with unerring skill, the 'lyre of mind,' and produced thence divine harmony" (Shelley 1996: 24). Adrian's kindness turns Verney's anger to friendship, and his discursive reasoning changes Verney's perspective on nature.

Thus, Verney feels he has just been admitted into a new existence. His conversion is humanist as well as civil, as he believes he attains the "intellectual and moral nature of man" in contrast with animals (Shelley 1996: 26). Clearly, the introduction to Adrian alters Verney's "ecological identity." Historically, the depiction of untamed nature had positive and negative aspects. While the wild represented God's power and nature's majesty, it could also imply the lower classes and native peoples who supposedly needed to be controlled in order to maintain civilization (Merchant 2003: 89). From a self-described "wolf-bred savage" (Shelley 1996: 15), a shepherd whose existence is at one with nature—especially its violent and disruptive forces— Verney emerges from Adrian's tutelage imbued with the vision and consciousness of a Romantic poet. Yet he compares this change to the European discovery of the American continent, seeking the wonder and enormity of meaning in the first sighting (Shelley 1996: 27). He expresses his experience in a visual metaphor, presented not as intellectual light but as an intensifica-

tion of sense, a new telescopic insight into the world's knowledge provided
by poetry and philosophy. The Cartesian extension of matter in space has
changed into a cognitive yet physical extension of Verney's personal vision.

As a political apprenticeship for the young man, Adrian procures a position for him as private secretary to the Ambassador to Vienna (Shelley 1996:
31). Verney then displays a more cultivated yet not unexpected perception of
nature. After his return he explains, "For my own part, since Adrian had first
withdrawn me from my selvatic wilderness to his own paradise of order and
beauty, I had been wedded to literature" (Shelley 1996: 122). As an aspiring
author, he seeks inspiration in the landscape. Nevertheless, his newly ac-
quired elite education and literary ambition have influenced his concept of
nature, derived from the Western Baconian narrative of conquest and mastery. Verney writes, "If I left the woods, the solemn music of the waving
branches, and the majestic temple of nature, I sought the vast halls of the
Castle, and looked over wide, fertile England, spread beneath our regal
mount, and listened the while to inspiring strains of music. At such times
solemn harmonies or spirit-stirring airs gave wings to my lagging thoughts,
permitting them, methought, to penetrate the last veil of nature and her God"
(Shelley 1996: 122–23). His colonizing perspective is mapped onto the English countryside in the semblance of female nature as a royal consort. Although the depiction of nature as female may reflect sacred and nurturing
aspects, Merchant cautions that these images are more likely to represent
"negative sexual, acquisitive, and exploitative connotations" (2003: 118–19).
The royalist idea has replaced both Verney's peasant revolt and Adrian's
Edenic imagination. In disloyalty to his own lived experience and to Adrian's
idealism, Verney's Romantic insight has been replaced by a more traditional
vista.

NATURE'S ROAD

The frontispiece of Alexander Pope's poem *An Essay on Man* depicts "im-
mortal man," the ancient sculpture of an envoy or Roman military man
perhaps, fallen from its pedestal, with a musical score and pipe nearby.
Drawn by Pope himself, the carved Latin letters of the now ironic inscription
on fame are obscured in shadow: SIC TRANSTE GLORIA MVND. In a
later version, the scene includes a man in worn-out nineteenth-century cloth-
ing with a print of the Prodigal Son in his hand, thoughtful amid broken
statuary (Mack 1950: xc). Supposedly a rake, he also seems much like Verney, the last man, alone in Rome at the end of the novel. After it appeared in
1733–1734, Pope's *Essay* was suspected of being a religiously and politically
unorthodox defense of Deism or "natural religion." Nevertheless, the poem
was resolutely on the side of the status quo. While Pope's final valorization

of the nation's strict hierarchy from servant to king, mirroring a "great chain of being," was not acceptable to Romantic republican values, the progress of the poem could easily be read in terms of unity in diversity. The moral and political philosophy expressed in the poem, "All Discord, Harmony, not understood" (Epistle I.X.291), originates in *concors discordia*—the classical idea that social harmony, like the harmony of the natural world, arises from the discord of diverse individual needs tempered by the benefits of cooperation and subordinated to the natural processes of the whole (Mack 1950: xxxiv–xxxv; Spitzer 1963: 40).[3] In this line, the complex relation between discourse and music seems resolved on the side of reason and self-knowledge. More than a metaphor, harmony from discord comprises a rhetoric of respect for all natural beings and the recognition of human limitations consistent with Shelley's ecofeminist interpretation.

Even though the characters in *The Last Man* closely resemble notable people in Shelley's life including Percy Shelley and Byron, their approaches to nature may not quite correspond with those of their real-life inspirations. Significantly, these viewpoints reveal the environmental philosophy that is the subject of the novel. Adrian and Raymond are often described as idealizations of the late poets. Yet, in addition to affectionate portrayals, more destructive aspects of their personalities emerge. In their responses to nature, the main characters each exemplify a variation on a theme from Pope's didactic poem. Mary Shelley adapts the fictional characters' motivations in order to represent modes of ecological thought, concepts that have subsequently been considered in contemporary ecocriticism. While some aspects of their ecological standpoints initially seem appropriate and ethical, Shelley's carefully constructed narrative demonstrates the ways in which each leads to disastrous personal, social, and environmental consequences.

In *An Essay on Man*, excessive pride or ambition often accompanies reason, while contrary passions may balance each other or be put in the service of virtues. The "ruling passion" can give one direction in life and a purpose in society, yet it may also become obsessive or harmful. Pope terms it "The Mind's disease" (Epistle II.III.138). An almost alchemical reaction occurs when Lord Raymond returns as the champion of Greek liberty and hero of Greek national songs and meets the young Earl of Windsor: "Adrian and Raymond now came into contact, and a spirit of aversion rose between them. Adrian despised the narrow views of the politician, and Raymond held in supreme contempt the benevolent visions of the philanthropist" (Shelley 1996: 38).

The contrast can be integrally described in terms of the characters' ecological identity.[4] Raymond's egocentric drive to mastery resembles the *Essay*'s synopsis of pride: "He looked on the structure of society as but a part of the machinery which supported the web on which his life was traced. The earth was spread out as a highway for him; the heavens built up as a canopy for him."[5] Still, he cannot master his own intense passions. Adrian has the more transcendent yet ecocentric worldview: "Adrian felt that he made a part of a great whole. He owned affinity not only with mankind, but all nature was akin to him . . . while he the focus only of this mighty mirror, felt his life mingle with the universe of existence." Although the two could not be more dissimilar, each nevertheless holds a universalizing natural philosophy— whether mechanist or Neoplatonic. It is Raymond who brings the storm that ruins Adrian's garden; Raymond, "the deliverer of Greece, the graceful soldier," inadvertently wins the affections of the Greek princess Evadne Zaimi from Adrian, whose health and composure are thus tragically shaken (Shelley 1996: 38–39).

Even after recovering from this emotional disturbance, Adrian remains unwell. On the return to Windsor through the countryside, he seeks solace in nature and rural life. Adrian's prospect is still inclusive of the diversity and equity of its human and nonhuman inhabitants. Yet Verney senses the effect of a more remote perspective as sounds from the far away villages are "harmonized by distance." Contemplating the sunset, Adrian expresses his thanks for creation: "A stately palace has God built for you, O man! and worthy are you of your dwelling! Behold the verdant carpet spread at our feet, and the azure canopy above; the fields of earth which generate and nurture all things, and the track of heaven, which contains and clasps all things" (Shelley 1996: 61–62). In contrast with Raymond's, Adrian's world is a verdant dwelling, not a highway. Yet his once free-spirited, holistic ecological identity has become tinged with mechanism and solemnity. Adrian (like Verney) echoes Pope's description of the original state of nature as Edenic: "In the same temple, the resounding wood, / All vocal beings hymn'd their equal God" (Epistle III.III.155–56). Finally, his reverie on the divine order of nature appears to be an expanded version of the Baconian objective to recover the earthly paradise. He proclaims the hope to eradicate sickness, hatred, and fear through the "omnipotent" will of man and dedicates his intellect to helping others (Shelley 1996: 63).

KNOWLEDGE AND POWER

According to Francis Bacon, "man's" body is like "a musical instrument of much and exquisite workmanship, which is easily put out of tune." Bacon approves of the identification of music and medicine with Apollo because of the affinity between the two vocations, since the endeavor of the physician is to "tune this harp of man's body that the harmony may be without all harshness or discord." However, he goes on to contend that while a lawyer or a ship's captain is evaluated in terms of skills and not by the outcome of the trial or success of the voyage, physicians and politicians cannot so readily demonstrate their capabilities and thus are judged according to the results. This does not seem appropriate to Bacon, as it may even favor an imposter instead of a virtuous, learned practitioner. "For who can know," he asks, "if a patient dies or recover, or if a state be preserved or ruined, whether it be art or accident?" (Bacon 1996b: 380–81).

This mystery in the correlation of music and medicine ultimately affects the entire civic body. "Does that voice no longer 'discourse excellent music'?" Verney exclaims in horror when he learns of Adrian's madness (Shelley 1996: 37). As he explains, the former queen had contrived to form Adrian's temperament and opinions to induce him to seek the restoration of the monarchy his father had abrogated. Thus, "By the application of praise, censure, and exhortation, she tried to seek and strike the fitting chords; and though the melody that followed her touch seemed discord to her, she built her hopes on his talents, and felt sure that she would at last win him" (Shelley 1996: 29). Unfortunately Adrian expressed his strongly egalitarian ideals before he had the ability to implement them. Instead his youthful and ardent republicanism alienated the rich and powerful, confounded other young people, and infuriated his mother (Shelley 1996: 38).

Like Hamlet, Adrian feels betrayed by his mother and abandoned by his presumed future spouse. When Guildenstern, along with Rosencrantz, arrives with his mother's summons, Hamlet challenges him to play the pipe.[6] Guildenstern refuses, and Hamlet insists, "'Tis as easy as lying" (3.2.340). Evidently, the phrase Verney has adapted from Hamlet, "discourse most eloquent music" (3.2.342), is not so much inexactly remembered from the play's context as made appropriate for Adrian. Certainly, eloquence has often been associated with excellence of character in the history of rhetoric. Yet, the contrast between Raymond's renown and Adrian's integrity is evident. Verney's allusion to *Hamlet* underscores Adrian's anger and resistance: "Call me what instrument you will, though you can / fret me, you cannot play upon me" (3.2.353–54). Eloquence in the service of his mother's intrigue is a deception that Adrian cannot accept.

In *The Last Man*, the Houses of Lords and Commons have been combined; however, the Senate is still divided into three coalitions: "aristocrats, democrats, and royalists." Verney's connections to Adrian, the Earl of Windsor, and to Lord Raymond allow him to observe the higher societal and governmental realms for himself. Verney was initially quite disturbed at the factionalism, believing the country to be nearing civil war. Regardless of Adrian's republicanism, the royalist party gained strength with Raymond's reappearance. Despite contention and ensuing social unrest, violence was avoided by the "cordial politeness and even friendship" of the leaders as the quarrel shifted from civil strife to politic rhetoric (Shelley 1996: 41–42). Behind the scenes, Raymond has arranged with the former queen to marry Adrian's sister Idris, and thus obtain the right to the earldom as a result of

Adrian's disordered emotional condition. He confides this arrangement to Verney: "Her power and my wit will rebuild the throne" (Shelley 1996: 46). By alluding to Bacon's most well-known aphorism as well as his famous wit, Raymond both characterizes and mocks the situation. He even seemingly transforms Bacon's Nature into a royal like the ex-queen, over whom he has an unexpected influence: "Human knowledge and human power meet in one; for where the cause is not known the effect cannot be produced. Nature to be commanded must be obeyed; and that which in contemplation is as the cause is in operation as the rule" (Bacon 1996a: 47). Raymond also reveals his imperialist plan to become greater than Napoleon and, should he become King, to league with the Greeks and conquer Constantinople (Shelley 1996: 48).

Raymond's opportunity to prove his rhetorical powers appears when Ryland, leader of the republicans, introduces a bill to make treasonous any attempt to alter the representative government. Of course, his purpose is to impede Raymond's "machinations" to restore the monarchy. In his grand speech, Ryland compares "the royal and republican spirit" (Shelley 1996: 49–50). The manner of their deliberations is similar to the humanist rhetorical exercise in comparison or *paragone*, contrasting rivals such as republic or monarchy, and nobility or meritocracy (Vickers 1989: 70). Ryland praises the positive effects of the government, reminding the assembly of their freedom and inspiring national pride. Then he warns against one who would put himself above his country and return England to strife (Shelley 1996: 49). When Raymond speaks, "his voice softly melodious, his manner soothing, his grace and sweetness came like the mild breathing of a flute, after the loud, organ-like voice of his adversary." Raymond subtly proposes an amendment to Ryland's resolution that an exception should be made if any of the royal family claim the throne, short of war. Concluding, he compares the "splendours of a kingdom" and stable government to republican commerce and political contests. Verney praises Raymond's ease and refinement, and especially "his voice, various as music, was like that enchanting" (Shelley 1996: 50-51). Ryland's measure fails, and by this maneuver Raymond considers his future as an "elected king" ensured. Privately, Raymond admits he is aware of the merits of Ryland's republicanism. He even tells Verney that he might have responded to reason in conversation, but the scene of public debate compelled him to predominate (Shelley 1996: 54).

DISCORD TO CONCORD

The critical theory of the Frankfurt School offers a vivid description of the complex relation between nature, human nature, and domination. From the first pages of *Eclipse of Reason*, Max Horkheimer considers the philosophic history of social harmony as he delineates the shift from objective to subjective reason, also referred to as critical and instrumental reason. For the early Greeks onward, reason was once supposed to be inherent in the structure of the universe and therefore in the human mind as well. While objective reason provided the foundation and ideals of human existence, subjective reason conferred the means of self-preservation and achieving more immediate interests. As hierarchical political and religious institutions were increasingly challenged, subjective or individual reason became the basis for a competitive economic system (Horkheimer 2004: 3–15).

According to Horkheimer, "Indeed, man's avidity to extend his power in two infinities, the microcosm and the universe, does not arise directly from his own nature, but from the structure of society" (2004: 74). He compares this to imperialism, which must be understood in peace and war as a result of a nation's internal conflicts rather than arising from any supposed national character. Attempts to dominate excluded nature originate in human relationships and not from essential human qualities. How then, Horkheimer asks, do inner nature and the natural world respond to oppression? The "revolt of nature" should be considered in terms of "psychological, political, and philosophical manifestations." Also, he asks, "Is it possible to void the conflict by a 'return to nature,' by a revival of old doctrines, or by the creation of new myths?" (Horkheimer 2004: 74–75).

This interconnected structure of psychology, politics, and philosophy is revealed in a discussion between Raymond and Verney following the debate in the Senate. Even though Verney disapproves of persuasive rhetoric in support of "visions of dominion, war, and triumph" (Shelley 1996: 57), he agrees to accompany Raymond to Windsor Castle. Along the way, Raymond introduces a new topic: "Philosophers have called man a microcosm of nature, and find a reflection in the internal mind for all this machinery visibly at work around us. This theory has often been a source of amusement to me; and many an idle hour have I spent, exercising my ingenuity in finding resemblances.[7] Does not Lord Bacon say that, 'the falling from a discord to a concord, which maketh great sweetness in music, hath an agreement with the affections, which are re-integrated to the better after some dislikes'?" (Shelley 1996: 54). Raymond refers to early modern scientific theory, juxtaposing Descartes' mind/body dualism and mechanistic concepts with Bacon's musical aphorism. While Descartes' view was that music moved the affections based on instrumental sound and culturally conditioned responses, Bacon found in music the same persuasive and ordering influence that rhetoric necessarily gives to law and religion (Hollander 1961: 176–80; 195–97).

Although their subsequent conversation takes the guise of an intellectual pastime, Raymond is preparing Verney, and himself, for an imminent decision. Reconsidering his choice of a marriage partner, he must decide if he will marry Idris for political advantage or wed Perdita based on his emotions.

The musical analogy Raymond quotes is from *Sylva Sylvarum*, Bacon's natural history (Bacon 1996d: 388–89).[8] Although the comparison occurs several times in Bacon's works, this is probably the most poetic instance. Perhaps it is such passages that contributed to his popularity during the Romantic era (Vickers 1968: 249).[9] In addition to acknowledging that music resembles varied emotions and that nations are partial to certain pieces, Bacon considers music's ability to prompt a range of conduct as well, from gentle to warlike. Nevertheless his purpose is to demonstrate that musical figures sometimes correspond with rhetorical ones and produce similar effects on the emotions, mind, and senses. While continual harmony compares with too much sweet taste, contrary emotions, as in musical compositions, are not divisive but become part of the overall impression (Bacon 1996d: 388–89).

In fact, Bacon makes his strongest case in *The Interpretation of Nature* that the comparison between musicians and rhetoricians is more than an intellectual pastime or allusion. He writes that instances of the fall from discord to accord and the delayed expectation or cadence reveal the relationship among knowledge of the parts and the whole (or the hermeneutic circle) in music, rhetoric, moral philosophy, policy, and so on, in their pleasant effects on the mind (Bacon 1996e: 228–31). Bacon explains that the interrupted cadence, or disrupted harmonic close, resembles the rhetorical figure he terms *praeter expectatum*. Even though the audience anticipates a resolution, the music elides it. While this is mildly disconcerting for the listeners, he also explains that there is enjoyment in the unexpected, or as he writes, in the deception (Bacon 1996d: 388–89).[10]

In true Baconian style, Raymond delays the revelation that he will propose to Perdita by contemplating seemingly unrelated resemblances from music and sailing. His explication of passion as a sea tossed by the winds indirectly refers to the discussion of the emotions and "medicining the mind," in *The Advancement of Learning*. In the context of mental health, Bacon considers the classic comparison of the people to the sea and the political orator to the wind in representative governments: Just as the people will be peaceful if not agitated, the mind will remain calm if not disturbed by the affections (Bacon 1996c: 23). His exemplification demonstrates the close connection between self-preservation and statecraft. Raymond's reference could be understood to implicate Adrian's radical politics in his emotional turmoil. Raymond then explains more directly that character is formed by education, interests, and the ways of the world, until opposed, like a thunderstorm, by a strong emotion such as "love, hate, or ambition." Thus his argument, which at first seems metaphysical and metaphorical, actually reveals a basis in the material circumstance of individual heredity and social construction. Appropriating the example in defense of Adrian's psychological "revolt of nature" and recovery, Verncy responds that one may nevertheless contend against the wind and even succeed—that rational choice is still possible.

Raymond disagrees; reverting to the musical analogy, he compares himself to a stringed instrument unable to rearrange his emotions or transpose his own thoughts into another key. Verney tersely replies, "Other men . . . may be better musicians" (Shelley 1996: 54–55).

Their indirect dispute over reason versus emotion develops into a statement on free will. Still they find that the once solid foundation that seemed so clearly to divide passion and rationality, necessity and freedom, has perceptibly altered from the days of Bacon and Descartes. Horkheimer finds that the "disease of reason" was always an element of civilization, as the propensity to dominate human and nonhuman nature. Yet, critical and instrumental reason can be reconciled with the realization that self-preservation is dependent on a respect for each individual (Horkheimer 2004: 119). He warns that any "theoretical harmony" (such as that represented by Raymond or even Adrian) can conceal power relations and complex social reality and thus be ideological as well as mythological. Therefore, philosophy must accord a society's ethics and aesthetics with its historical actuality in order to move forward (Horkheimer 2004: 123).

ROMANTIC NATURE

In *Discordant Harmonies*, Daniel Botkin identifies three ecological belief systems: nature as divine order, organic, and mechanistic. The concept of divine order and the machine metaphor posit both the constancy of nature and the significant role of human beings within it. In contrast, the organic image emphasizes change (as growth and decay) that humans cannot avoid (Botkin 1990: 12–13). Yet he asserts that these familiar ideas about nature actually prevent us from dealing effectively with the realities. Concepts of nature as divine order or as machine function similarly in terms of representing regular laws or equilibrium. In these views, humans can serve either to perfect the order of nature or to disrupt it. Inevitably, beliefs about nature reflect cultural inconsistencies (Botkin 1990: 109–10). Both Adrian's ecocentric and Raymond's egocentric understanding of nature incorporate an expectation of stability and progressive improvement in human well-being.

The characters do not reconcile the damaging effects of their beliefs about nature until it is too late. The ensemble of friends retreats to the rural neighborhood of Windsor Castle to enjoy years of quiet companionship and marital and family happiness. Adrian never marries but remains close to Verney and Idris, and Perdita and Raymond. Nevertheless, the times call for Raymond's leadership; with Adrian's and Verney's support, he returns to public life and becomes Lord Protector. He sets aside his military ambitions and actively pursues the Baconian project of intermingling nature and science to improve the lives of all. However, the organic belief about nature becomes the principle that will suffuse the rest of the narrative, as disrupted natural forces supersede philosophic ideals. While classical aesthetics usually centered on perfection in the form of symmetry and balance, in the nineteenth century the Romantics affirmed the organic perspective. Botkin sees this as a rejection of the empirical science and mechanical worldview of the previous century and also an appreciation of the sublime nature of distant locales. The transformation from a divinely ordered universe to awareness of the majestic power of nature also represents a change in science from an interest in structure to the study of natural processes (Botkin 1990: 95–97).

This transition in worldview in the novel originates in the breakup of the marriage of Raymond and Perdita. Raymond encounters Evadne again when she submits architectural drawings for a new national gallery; he feels compassion for her illness and poverty, and their attraction is renewed. He neglects not only his marriage but the government as well. When he does not arrive at the festival his wife has arranged in honor of his first anniversary as Protector, she realizes he is having an affair. Her own inner change is reflected in the autumn weather: "'All things go on,' thought Perdita, 'all things proceed, decay, and perish!'" Confirming an organic belief, she realizes that even though the heavens are considered eternal, everything is in fact mutable and constantly in flux. More than that, Perdita senses that the infidelity of the nation's leader is just the beginning of ever increasing disorders. Momentarily near madness, she utters her prophetic statement (a recurring motif—or fugue, similar to the celestial symbolism of *The Creation* and Percy Shelley's *Epipsychidion*): "[T]he sun itself, sovereign of the sky, . . . deserts his throne, and leaves his dominion to night and winter. Nature grows old, and shakes in her decaying limbs,—creation has become bankrupt! What wonder then, that eclipse and death have led to destruction the light of thy life, O Perdita!" (Shelley 1996: 106). If individuals are a microcosm of the greater cosmos, then the declining condition of the creation is also evident.

As Botkin implies, the success of the domination of nature also has adverse effects; and concepts of nature inherited from the Greco-Roman, medieval, Renaissance, and industrial eras must be rethought (Botkin 1990: 189–90). In place of fundamental principles of divine order and mechanism, he proposes a contemporary alternative that combines the organic model of natural change and a technological metaphor of conservancy. The solution he suggests is to obtain more knowledge and make use of information technologies. He asks, "If we do not understand the true nature of populations, biological communities, and ecosystems, how can we expect to husband them wisely?" (Botkin 1990: 191). Botkin thus alludes to Bacon's "marriage between Mind and Nature"[11] in terms of a science with origins in Baconian methods of observation and induction. However, the objective is to understand and adapt to natural processes instead of attempting to force nature into a preordained ideal state without a realistic concern for the consequences.

CONCLUSION

Near the close of the novel's first volume, Raymond rejoins his friends at a musical gathering similar to those Mary Shelley attended at the Novello's. He discusses his administrative policies for new buildings and improved education for the poor with Verney and Adrian, yet once again arguing with Adrian. Perdita has been studying music: her voice is "without much power, but with a great deal of sweetness." At her insistence, the melodies are from Mozart's light operas. When Raymond performs songs of love and betrayal from *The Marriage of Figaro* and *Don Giovanni*, his "concord of sound with its dissonance of expression" dismays Perdita. Now, as she describes herself, wedded to despair, she finds slight comfort in her brother's consolation, his words distant like "the remembered sounds of forgotten music" (Shelley 1996: 108–9). Words become part of an emotional performance, while music alone still conveys a genuine emotive power. As Shelley explained in a letter from October 1823, "I am becoming very fond of instrumental music" since a listener's thoughts provide her own lyrics, "if it be not more in harmony with the notes at least is more so with one's tone of mind" (1980: 393). Shelley's musical appreciation corresponds with the Romantic transition from vocal to instrumental pieces and from rhetorically influenced to organic musical composition.

After this evening their lives will never be the same. Raymond resigns the Protectorate, and he convinces Adrian to join the fighting in Greece with him. After their arrival, the gradual advance of the Greek forces overturns the armed truce (another connotation of *concordia discors*) between the Western Europeans and the armies of Turkey and its allies. A band follows the march, playing martial music at dawn and solemn laments or hymns in the evening; and then until the final chapters the novel's music fades away (Shelley 1996: 141). Each of the characters is eventually conquered by his or her pride and ambition. They find themselves involved in a military conflict that will irrevocably lead to the dissemination of plague to all the nations.

Although Botkin's discordant harmonies better explain the processes of nature and Merchant's partnership ethics provide a sound non-gendered basis for the relationship between human and nonhuman nature, many ecofeminists may find that the contingencies of human interactions need further interpretation. According to Luce Irigaray, war can be an incongruous attempt to restore order or to initiate different options for the future. She advocates the establishment of "an ethics of the couple" to mediate relations between individuals as well as nations. She writes, "Wars break out when peoples move too far from their natural possibilities, when abstract energy builds up so much that it can no longer be controlled by subjects or reduced to one or more concrete responsibilities" (Irigaray 1993: 5). Certainly Mary Shelley was writing about the intense psychological connections between the person-

120 *Vicky L. Adams*

al, political, and environmental spheres. Irigaray's statement is congruent with the themes of *The Last Man*. The options inherent in discord and/or the need for the harmony of order must be tempered by respect for the human and nonhuman world. A new dialectic for natural and social harmony should not be based on the synthesis of opposites in a masculinist mythology. Any arrangement of voices must be carefully composed in order to allow for difference without cognitive dissonance. The reconciliation of nature includes not only mutual respect but also emotional fidelity to oneself and others.

NOTES

1. Leo Spitzer attributes the decrease of references to natural and social "world harmony" to the Enlightenment or Max Weber's "disenchantment of the world." The music metaphor was replaced by the metaphor of light as cultural concepts changed (Spitzer 1963: 75–76).

2. This is not quite as anachronistic or implausible as it first seems. As Brian Vickers states, "We can posit that Dr Johnson and Burke had essentially the same education as Hooker and Bacon, and it was not till the reform of the curricula and the rise of modern subjects in the nineteenth century that the rhetorical education becomes reduced to one simply in classics, one subject amongst many" (1989: 54).

3. 'Till jarring int'rests of themselves create

    Th'according music of a well-mix'd State.

    Such is the World's great harmony, that springs

       From Order, Union, full Consent of things! (*An Essay on Man*. Epistle III

293–96)

4. Adrian's "ethic of care" is juxtaposed with Raymond's "heroic ethics." Marti Kheel explains, "Learning to respond to nature in caring ways is not an abstract exercise in reasoning. It is, above all, a form of psychic and emotional health. Heroic ethics cannot manufacture health out of the void of abstraction. Psychic and emotional health cannot be manufactured at all. It can only be nurtured through the development of a favorable environment or context within which it can grow. The moral 'climate' must be right" (Kheel 1993: 260).

5. Shelley alludes to the following passage in Pope's *An Essay on Man*:

    Ask for what end the heav'nly bodies shine,

    Earth for whose use? Pride answers,"'Tis for mine:

    . . . .

    "For me health gushes from a thousand springs;

    "Seas roll to waft me, suns to light me rise;

    "My footstool earth, my canopy the skies."

    But errs not Nature from this gracious end,

    From burning suns when livid deaths descend,

    When earthquakes swallow, or when tempests sweep

    Towns to one grave, whole nations to the deep? (Epistle I.V.131–32; 138–44)

In these lines Pride appropriates God's voice in Isaiah (66.1) and exhibits the presumption of well-being while disregarding effects of plague and natural disaster when these occur elsewhere. In addition to Milton's *Paradise Lost*, Isaiah's prophecy strongly influenced Shelley's vision of natural apocalypse and future restoration in *The Last Man*.

6. In an earlier conversation with Guildenstern, Hamlet alludes to Isaiah: "This most excellent canopy, the air, look / you, this brave o'erhanging firmament, this majestical / roof fretted with golden fire—why, it appears no other / thing to me than a foul and pestilent congregation of / vapours" (2.2.297–301).

7. Although Bacon did not endorse the alchemical doctrine of celestial and earthly correspondences based on the macrocosm-microcosm theory (Bacon 1996b: 379–80), he did recommend "the investigation and observation of the resemblances and analogies of things" in order to demonstrate the "unity of nature" (Bacon 1996a: 167). This type of comparison infuses Bacon's rhetoric; Shelley's narrative makes use of the technique instead to emphasize inconsistencies and instability.

8. Shelley read *Sylva Sylvarum* in 1822. She had connections with Bacon's nineteenth-century editors. Basil Montague, who represented Percy Shelley in a failed attempt to gain custody of his children by his first marriage, published his first volume of Bacon's collected works in 1825. Interestingly, Montague was involved in controversy after defending Bacon's character in print (Mathews 1996: 22–23). Later, Shelley's son was acquainted with Leslie Ellis, and James Spedding was related to her daughter-in-law. Both men were to become editors of the 1870s edition (Sunstein 1989: 130, 251, 378).

9. Bacon's rhetoric has been the subject of recent intense critical debate between ecofeminists and traditional Bacon scholars. (See the forum on Carolyn Merchant's *The Death of Nature* in *Isis*, September 2006. Articles critiquing and defending Bacon by Merchant and Vickers respectively appear in *Journal of the History of Ideas*, January 2008.) In *Frankenstein* and *The Last Man* in particular, Shelley reveals the contradictions inherent in Bacon's program to dominate nature.

10. For a discussion of this passage in Bacon, see Butler (1980: 60–62) and Vickers (1996: 203–4). Feminist musicologist Susan McClary (2002) outlines the terminology of masculine and feminine cadences in *Feminine Endings: Music, Gender, and Sexuality*.

11. For a discussion of feminist and ecofeminist positions on this subject and the nature/culture dichotomy in Bacon as well as Descartes, see Arneil (1999: 86–88).

Afterword

Ecofeminism: The Ironic Philosophy

Jeffrey A. Lockwood

Ralph Waldo Emerson, who might be considered an ecofeminist through only the most convoluted of conceptual paths, arguably set the conceptual stage for ecofeminism when he wrote (1983: 265):

> A foolish consistency is the hobgoblin of little minds, adored by little states-men, philosophers and divines. With consistency a great soul has simply noth-ing to do. He may as well concern himself with his shadow on the wall. Speak what you think today in hard words, and tomorrow speak what tomorrow thinks in hard words again, though it contradict every thing you said today.

Any sophisticated system of thought that authentically engages the complexity of the world will sometimes contradict itself. It seems to me that only the purely abstract endeavors, such as formal logic, have the luxury of consistency for they don't bear the burden of having to work on messy problems that truly matter to actual people and other living beings. And this is why I suggest that ecofeminism is, at its core, an endeavor rich in irony.

As an ecologist and environmental philosopher who enjoys a joint appointment with the MFA program in creative writing at the University of Wyoming, I can offer an uncommon, if not unique, perspective on ecofeminist literary criticism. Of course, there are many literary ecocritics with joint appointments, but few (if any) have extensive academic experience in the science of ecology. And given Emerson's engagement with philosophy, nature, and literature, it seems appropriate to reflect on this provocative and insightful book through the lens of contradiction or more specifically irony. The preceding chapters are far too elegant and complicated to recapitulate in a few words, so I've chosen a set of important conceptual conflicts that are vividly exemplified by the authors. Each represents an important idea raised by the author, if not always the central theme, that piqued my ecological and philosophical sense of contrariness.

My intention is not at all mean-spirited; ironies may be wicked, but I am not. Rather, I take seriously ecofeminist claims, and through irony hope to explore their edges, limits, and applications to discover the contexts in which they work and fail. The authors' complex literary insights provide a rich source for a reader who is genuinely trying to appreciate ecofeminist scholars—people who speak what they "think today in hard words . . . [even] though it contradict."

THE IRONIES OF ECOFEMINISM

Caring: What Are the Right Things and Amounts?

Monique LaRocque's chapter on the Decadent period, with particular attention to J. K. Huysmans' *A Rebours*, makes a compelling case that life is tragically impoverished when experience is abstracted from authentic relationships and the natural world. LaRocque provides a convincing interpretation of the character Des Esseintes as a man who cares not at all for nature. His escape into aestheticism comes with the price of accepting a shallow and vacuous existence. But as persuasive as LaRocque's analysis is, this ecofeminist view provides a particularly rich irony. That is, ecofeminists advocate a pluralistic ethic of caring, but they seem to reject our caring for human creations. For example, Des Esseintes buys and decorates a turtle to complement his oriental rug, so that a piece of art rather than a living being is the focus of his concern. LaRocque is unmoved by this expression of caring—a position that adds credibility to the ecofeminist project. Rather than just any sort of caring being sufficient for a moral life, one also must care about the right things. And it appears that rugs and other human artifices are the wrong things.

Ecofeminists also contend that we can, and should, care for ourselves. This position is rarely nuanced, but much to her credit LaRocque provides intellectual clarity through her interpretation of *A Rebours*. She makes evident that the narcissistic care that Des Esseintes lavishes on himself—which entails isolation from both the natural world and fellow humans—is excessive. So it is evident that ethical failings can be both qualitative (caring for the wrong sorts of things) and quantitative (caring too much for even the right sorts of things).

In bringing together these more complex considerations of ecofeminist caring LaRocque maintains that "Both [Decadents and the bourgeois] . . . [sought] to replace the natural/organic with artificiality." While wholesale replacement is problematic, at least some ecofeminists endorse partial replacement (e.g., substitution of natural habitats with farmlands can be virtuous, according to the argument developed by Werden [2001]). LaRocque has substantially deepened and complicated the caring ethic of ecofeminism. And while this might evoke a contradiction (if we reject dualism and see humans as natural, then what does it mean to replace the organic with the artificial?), it also represents an exciting maturation of the field.

So it is that LaRocque has opened two lines of sophistication. Perhaps the easier problem to solve is that of immoderate care (ecofeminism taps into Aristotle's notion of "virtue as moderation" as will be seen in a later consideration of LaRocque's chapter). The tougher problem for ecofeminists is that of caring about the wrong kinds of things. It remains a most fruitful line of research to answer explicitly the question that LaRocque raises implicitly: How do we know what things we ought to care about?

Karen Warren (2000) provides criteria of care, including: a cognitive awareness of the subject's needs, the passage through developmental phases of concern, and the non-necessity of either reciprocity or feeling for the subject of care. These standards do not preclude a conservator caring for the *Mona Lisa*, a collector protecting ancient coins, a mechanic restoring a '57 Chevy, or Des Esseintes attending to his oriental rug. However, LaRocque suggests that, "because [Des Esseintes] perceives [his environment] as artificial and removed, he has no attachment to it. This attitude of indifference facilitates the potential for exploiting nature and is an attitude shared by his bourgeois contemporaries in the increasingly industrialized world." This might well be one line of reasoning but it does not necessarily follow that what is artificial can be exploited, nor is it empirically the case that we are indifferent to artificial things (e.g., historic buildings, the Statue of Liberty, and the Gutenberg Bible). Des Esseintes says, "The time is undoubtedly come when her [Nature's] productions must be superseded by art," and the ecofeminist counters that our care for natural objects ought to trump our care for works of art. But is this always the case? If I must choose between crushing a rock or Michelangelo's *David*, it seems defensible that I'd choose to reduce the former to rubble.

The ecofeminist ethic of care, which is explicated by Nel Noddings (2003), represents a genuinely novel and compelling approach to morality. And the principle of culturally sensitive, locally contextual, pluralistic values seems quite plausible (worries about countenancing degenerate relativism notwithstanding). But we are left with the problem of why it is wrong to care for artificial things, presuming that the artificial-natural dualism is valid and useful (more about that later). LaRocque provides some hints as to possible solutions. For example, valuing a turtle as an accoutrement to an oriental rug is a moral mistake. Caring about turtles and rugs is defensible, but the error comes in why we care—treating living beings solely as means to our ends is the sort of moral mistake that lies at the heart of Kant's deontology, although his concern was limited to rational beings.

But perhaps caring should not be circumscribed so quickly. Caring might be best understood along the lines that a minister I knew proposed in speaking of same-sex marriages. Once we have a world in which there is enough love, then we can worry about whether we're loving the right people. So a lack of caring—whatever the origin—rather than wrongheaded caring, would seem to be the greater problem for ecofeminists at this time. Indeed, this would seem to echo the concern that LaRocque raises in her analysis.

Ethics: Holistic Universals or Reductionistic Particulars?

Eric Otto's chapter on ecofeminist science fiction explores the ways in which this literature delves into form and function of a compassionate, egalitarian world. The authors in this genre obviously struggle to avoid feminist clichés in their stories, but Otto's chapter points to the emergent irony. Ecofeminism seeks contextual, local, and nuanced views but tends to reduce some important and complex ideas to simple terms. Let's first consider some of these problematical reductionisms and then suggest why at least one ecofeminist reduction which Otto and others countenance is critical to the viability of this endeavor. Then we'll turn to how Otto manages to navigate a conceptually compelling path through ecofeminism without being cast upon the rocks of essentialism or swept away by the currents of particularism—what philosophers might classically see as the dual hazards of realism and nominalism (Reiners and Lockwood 2009).

Otto and others allude to Warren's (2000) "logic of domination," which reduces the complicated relationship between women and nature to implausible terms (see Levin and Levin 2001). In short, the argument is that if I perceive that A (women) is like B (nature), and if I can justifiably do X (harm) to A, it follows that I can do X to B. Even if we stipulate that A is like B in some ways and that we are justified in doing X to A, it might well be the case that B differs from A in some relevant way that would prohibit me from doing X to B. The "logic of domination" is just too simple to subsume the nature of exploitation.

Another common simplification in ecofeminist writings is the muddling, if not equating, of domination with oppression. In this case, Warren (2000) comes to the rescue in providing a nuanced view that distinguishes these two actions. In short, domination occurs when one adopts a position of superiority from which one then controls another, while oppression occurs when this control is imposed contrary to the will of another. This nuanced understanding allows the possibility of justified domination (e.g., a parent controlling a child's access to electrical outlets) and disallows the possibility of oppressing many natural entities (e.g., a pond, which is not oppressed by restoration because it does not want to be stagnant). Much of ecofeminism would become much clearer if Warren's distinctions were more widely recognized.

Another reductionistic move is to equate dualisms (or any form of qualitative distinction) with axiological hierarchies. While it is true that valuing A over B entails A differing from B, it does not follow that if I distinguish A from B then I must place some greater value on either A or B—they could simply be different. We can recognize difference as difference and nothing more.

The final simplification comes when ecofeminists offer various solutions to the patriarchal claim that Women = Nature, Nature = Inferior, therefore Women = Inferior. As aptly summarized by Warren (2000), responses include changing the first premise to either Women ≠ Nature or Women = Men = Nature or changing the second premise to either Nature = Superior or Women ≠ Inferior. All of these moves fail to recognize that Women are (un)like Nature and Men in particular situations. And it is this contextualism that obviates the need to reduce Women to being either utterly dissimilar or entirely the same as Men or Nature.

While these simplifications are problematical, there is a dualistic reduction that prevents ecofeminism from lapsing into vacuous relativism. Much to their credit, Otto and most other ecofeminists recognize that when it comes to acting, there is an important difference between good and bad. As subtle and locally contextual as they might seek to be, ecofeminists argue for some clear and simple positions: freedom is better than oppression, respect is better than denigration, justice is better than unfairness, and equality is better than sexism. There might be multifarious factors that condition how we respond, but in the end it is still possible and necessary to distinguish—however simple this might be—good acts from bad acts.

Otto manages to sustain critical moral distinctions while avoiding naïve simplifications. In so doing, he identifies and develops a rather sophisticated approach to ecofeminism that attends to hierarchies of all sorts, including but not limited to patriarchy. He sees in science fiction elements of core principles while recognizing the need to move beyond dichotomous views that undermine the ecofeminist project. For example, in his analysis of Joan Slonczewski's *A Door Into Ocean*, Otto is sympathetic with the moral position that freedom is preferable to oppression and sharing is more virtuous than conquest. But he shows that science fiction can also challenge feminist essentialism. The most vicious soldier in the oppressor's army is a female Chief of Staff, and a teenage boy joins the Sharer culture. In analyzing Slonczewski's characters, Otto makes the case that rather than being some biological or genetic essence of men and women, militarism and pacifism are socially conditioned—a position that provides a much more plausible, if complicated, account of the world (however, the view that violence is constructed is a problematical oversimplification, given the contribution of genetics to this aspect of human behavior).

Essentialism: Bad for the Goose but Good for the Gander?

Theda Wrede explores the ecofeminist effort to subvert the Western myth through the writing of Barbara Kingsolver. Wrede's analysis is provocative in suggesting an irony overlooked by many in her field. That is, ecofeminists decry essentialism but often frame non-feminist works in essentialist terms. Indeed, Wrede notes that Kingsolver's novel *Animal Dreams* presents an utterly predictable storyline based on stereotypically essential qualities of masculine (anti)heroes. Kingsolver's book is set in the Southwest, so let us take for our target myth the archetypal genre of the Western and in particular the character of the cowboy. This classic hero is readily but superficially framed in terms of being a violent character deplorably lacking in intersubjectivity. But Wrede's analysis suggests that if we look more deeply for virtuous qualities (e.g., relationality), a reader might find portrayals that refute ecofeminist essentialism.

As I've argued previously (Lockwood 2008), there is a pervasive oversimplification of Westerns. This contemporary myth essentializes the cowboy as being devoid of relationality, a concern that Wrede raises about masculine heroes in our cultural myths. However, a careful reading of Westerns (or an attentive viewing of films) reveals a rather more complex character. In fact, the cowboy is often portrayed as protecting the weak, sick, injured, and vulnerable. He has a tough exterior but a soft heart when it comes to those who have been unjustly treated. Moreover, the cowboy is fiercely loyal—a quality that belies the claim that he lacks intersubjective sensibilities.

Wrede portrays male settlers as destroying nature and accruing a sense of guilt for having penetrated and desecrated virginal land. This might well be an element of agrarian myths, but the cowboy lives in intimate connection to the land. He experiences nature's extremes and accepts the land on its own terms, without imposing anthropomorphic interpretations. As such, he rejects the land-grabbing tactics of the Eastern, absentee owner who does not understand the people or places that are objects of exploitation. The cowboy does not seek material wealth but aspires to become rich in experiences and relationships—a condition that seems rather consonant with ecofeminism.

Of course, the cowboy is a peripatetic hero, so can he truly come to understand a particular, natural setting? In many stories, itinerancy is a youthful phase that ends with his settling into a place—a locale that is rarely pretty in superficial terms but genuinely beautiful if understood deeply. This maturation into a paradoxical relationship of otherness and togetherness with fellow humans and the natural world is vividly portrayed by John Wayne in *The Cowboys* and by the title character in Louis L'Amour's *Conagher*.

Wrede advocates a shift of cultural values from separateness to relationality, but this is presumably not a call for wholesale rejection of individualism
and the adoption of totalizing communtarianism. Ecofeminists, for the most
part, advocate a balanced perspective, a kind of Golden Mean that seeks the
virtue in caring for both oneself and others. And one can read the cowboy
myth as reflecting this search for autonomy and compassion, with the hero
cultivating a sense of fierce independence while valuing loyalty and protecting the vulnerable.

The ecofeminist seeks the wisdom found in alternative perspectives, as
reflected in Wrede's contention that "what is *also* at issue is the respectful
treatment of cultures themselves." And Kingsolver envisions her ecofeminist
myth as countering the cultural trauma of the West through a reciprocal
caring for the land. But perhaps a deeper and more charitable reading of the
Western myth should be included in "the respectful treatment" of cultural
stories. In the cowboy, one might even find a hero manifesting many of the
qualities that Kingsolver and other ecofeminist writers seek as antidotes to
the desecration of the land and the exploitation of people. If so, Wrede
deserves our admiration for having opened the door to a self-critical reflection on ecofeminist essentialism which makes such a reading of the Western
possible.

Values: Intrinsic or Relational?

Vicky Adams elegantly explores how musical harmony can be used as a
metaphor to understand Romantic prose and, in particular, Mary Shelley's
The Last Man. Embedded within the literary critique is the question of intrinsic qualities: Are the discordant harmonies within stories, the complex relationships within societies, and the intricate exchanges within ecosystems
present in and of themselves, or are they latent potentials that are realized
only when perceived and acted upon? The most fundamental ecofeminist
claim in this regard is that nature has intrinsic value (Warren 2000: 74). And
this gives rise to the irony in which ecofeminists takes intrinsic value to be
axiomatic, but apparently overlook that such a quality is contrary to relationality.

Much to her credit, Adams eschews the interpretation of Francis Bacon as
ecofeminism's enemy, representing all that is deplorable about the scientific
venture of reducing and dominating nature. While Bacon was an objectivist,
his advocacy of science was driven by a profound concern for human suffering which defined his experience in seventeenth-century England (ecofeminists advocate interpreting the lives of people in their historical and geographic context). Rather than depending on authorities to reveal the truth, Bacon
viewed science as a radically egalitarian epistemology that was available to
all people. The qualities of the natural world could be known to anyone, if

the proper methods were employed. But, one might ask, is intrinsic value one of these objective qualities?

If there is intrinsic value, then its existence is independent of our relationship to the natural world—we are at best passive instruments that can be calibrated to detect this value (or mistuned so as to overlook this quality). An intrinsic value is simply "there" and would exist whether or not anyone ever recognized its existence. Aside from the philosophical problems (e.g., does everything have intrinsic value; how do we know which things have it; do some things have more of it than others; if everything has intrinsic value then do we act any differently than if nothing had it?), it seems that ecofeminism has built its foundations on a principle that is ultimately non-relational and objectivist. Such is the nature of an internally ironic philosophy.

Objectivity: Does Science Foster or Avoid Domination?

Ecofeminism is, to some extent, irrevocably linked to the science of ecology, at least insofar as many of the concerns raised by ecofeminists arise from the findings of ecologists. In Marnie Sullivan's chapter on Rachel Carson's books about the sea, we are thrust into the ironic situation in which ecofeminism castigates science as coldly detached rationalism when it is science's objective approach that avoids the domineering and oppressive imposition of ourselves onto the world.

Sullivan provides an interesting disquisition on the concept of ecological imprisonment which is interpreted as a metaphor for transgressing social boundaries. If this was Carson's intention, then it might seem surprising that not all allusions to captivity are portrayed negatively in her sea books. In these cases, Carson's lack of subjective judgment concerning the goodness or badness of being a captive might simply reflect a scientist's studious and cultivated effort to be objective—to simply allow the natural world to be what it is, without imposing human approbation or condemnation.

Elsewhere in her chapter, Sullivan affirms the virtue of a scientific engagement with the natural world, although not in the classical terms that a scientist might immediately recognize. For example, she notes that Carson has an affinity for ambiguity in her work which mirrors this quality in the life forms she studies at ecological margins. This withholding of judgment such that one resists imposing a particular framework is the stuff of good science, as the investigator allows nature to be experienced on its own terms instead of making it "ours." And when Carson "promotes strategies that engage senses associated with body knowledge [of gulls]" as a viable alternative to the mental knowledge that humans presume is the pinnacle of the living world, she is reflecting the discipline of the scientist, who does not presume a grand teleology for ecology or evolution. Likewise, rather than framing the world in anthropocentric terms, "Carson encourages readers to look actively and use a strategy that engages other perspectives when necessary in order to do so." This way of seeing nature is standard (and damn good) advice to students of animal behavior and ecology. Sullivan perceptively recognizes that when Carson engages the natural world, it is "with the expectation that she will meet subjects," but there is a further, unspoken quality. That is, as a good scientist who understood the virtues of objectivity, Carson met her subjects on their own terms.

Context: Does History Matter for Ecofeminism Itself?

Richard Magee offers a stimulating and incisive analysis of the ecological views expressed by Rachel Carson and Barbara Kingsolver. The latter is seen as having built on the work of the former, and revealing this historical thread is a valuable contribution to our understanding of environmentalism. But it is important to continue to map the path for which Magee has laid these two vitally important waypoints. Magee was limited by space, so Carson's environmental ethic seems to arise *de novo* (i.e., no preceding sources for her inspiration are suggested). While Magee is surely aware that Carson relied on her (mostly male) predecessors, it is also the case that ecofeminism-from-nowhere is common in the literature. And this reflects a rather ironic situation in which ecofeminists emphasize the importance of socio-historical context but seem to overlook their own conceptual roots. So let's take this opportunity to continue Magee's admirable project in the spirit of ecofeminism and consider the plausible origins for Rachel Carson's work.

Before we begin however, it is worth noting that the link between Carson's environmental ethic and the ecofeminist values that followed (e.g., those implicit in Kingsolver's work) is compelling but not unproblematic. The vast majority of *Silent Spring*, for example, appeals to the instrumental value of nature while ecofeminism largely rejects this as a basis for ethics and insists on there being intrinsic value. Unfortunately, Carson never makes explicit whether she ascribes to such an axiology. Her ambiguous value system might best be understood as reflecting the approach taken by her predecessor—Aldo Leopold.

Some thirteen years before *Silent Spring*, Leopold's *A Sand County Almanac* laid out a compelling argument for an ethic which changed "the role of *Homo sapiens* from conqueror of the land-community to plain member and citizen of it" (1968: 204). Such a view seems eminently compatible with ecofeminism and entirely consistent with Carson's perspective. Indeed like her, Leopold was also frustratingly vague as to whether nature had intrinsic value. It seems that both he and Carson saw that the best way to persuade the people to take action against environmental degradation was to show how such opposition was in the public's enlightened self-interest. Leopold and Carson each cared deeply for a particular ecosystem (the sand counties of

Wisconsin and the seas around us), and through a scientifically informed and emotionally unapologetic series of experiences they both argued for protecting their treasured places.

Whether Carson read Leopold's work or not (Lear 1997), his environmental ethic provided an intellectual foundation for ecofeminism. At the very least, his contention that "a thing is right when it tends to preserve the integrity, stability, and beauty of the biotic community. It is wrong when it tends otherwise" was in the air, and Carson echoed his thoughts when she wrote of "the integrity of the environment," "the stability of nature," and "places of beauty" (Carson 2002: 2, 74–75).

Magee's assertion that Carson "reimagined a new connection between humans and nature" is a powerful way of summarizing her lasting contribution to environmentalism. In fact, Magee's having identified the importance of a qualitative shift in perspective—"a new connection"—serves as an incisive distillation of how scientists can contribute to humanity. And in this light, it is important to consider that Carson *re*imagined the human-nature connection as one of a highly rarified set of thinkers in the life sciences who have variously expressed this concept for more than 150 years.

In 1837, a year after the voyage of the *Beagle*, Charles Darwin wrote in his notebook (in Eiseley 1958: 352), "If we choose to let conjecture run wild, then animals, our fellow brethren in pain, disease, suffering and famine—our slaves in the most laborious works, our companions in our amusements—they may partake of our origin in one common ancestor—we may be all melted together." In her chapter in this book, Marnie Sullivan astutely notes that Carson's prose causes the reader to understand that humans are not of central importance. But if historical context matters in ecofeminism, then we should recognize that Carson was not working in isolation. Rather, she was a vital link in a long chain of scholars who have struggled against hubris. It is important to understand that while Carson can be seen as passing the baton of humility onto the likes of Arne Naess and the deep ecology movement, the baton had been passes for centuries. Roughly speaking, the challenge to anthropocentrism might be said to have begun with Galileo Galilei (who removed Earth from the cosmological center), then passed to Darwin (who removed humans from the teleological center), and was thereafter expressed by a lineage of ecologists leading up to Leopold (who removed humans from the ecological center) and then Carson. Her contribution was not so much the originality of her axiology as it was her political courage in a time of enormous human arrogance—a period in which we were at grave risk of dropping the baton. And for that, we all owe Carson our enduring gratitude.

Revolution: Does Ecofeminism Reject or Reflect Traditional Morality?

In LaRocque's ecofeminist critique of *A Rebours*, recall that Des Esseintes' flaw was not that he cared for himself but that he did so immoderately, indeed to such an extent that he became utterly self-absorbed. In short he lacked the classical virtues of humility, proportionality, and empathy. This understanding of the character serves to highlight an intriguing irony: Ecofeminism sees itself as breaking with the Western philosophical tradition but echoes the ancient Greek concept of *eudaimonia*. For Socrates and his successors, *eudaimonia* or "happiness" was a matter of cultivating the good life in accord with the virtues. Let's begin with another literary analysis from an ecofeminist perspective that perhaps even more vividly illustrates the connection between postmodern and ancient virtues, and then we'll turn to how LaRocque's insights allow ecofeminism to apparently break with tradition.

Werden (2001) took on the challenge of understanding agriculture in terms of ecofeminism by using Edna Ferber's *So Big* to show how farming can be a sensitive and responsible endeavor. Rather than the capital-intensive, industrial model that is usually taken to constitute modern food production, Selina (the main character) cultivates the land and her life in accord with what she takes to be ultimately worthwhile: leisure, color, travel, books, music, diverse people, and work that you love. These may not be identical to Aristotle's list (honesty, pride, friendliness, wittiness, rational judgment, mutual friendships, and scientific knowledge), but the point is that the ecofeminist heroine seeks a complex set of complementary experiences necessary for deep and authentic happiness. Neither the fictional farmer nor the ancient Greek believed that honor, wealth, and power were proper human aspirations. Rather, we are to seek genuine excellence (*arête*) in our lives, drawing from and realizing our individual potentials.

In the *Nicomachean Ethics*, Aristotle describes the central virtue of moderation. Courage, for example, is a matter of finding the mean between cowardice and rashness. As much as Des Esseintes fails to moderate his valuation of self and others, Selina succeeds in carefully balancing quality and quantity of her farm products. She falls prey neither to marketing a few gorgeous bunches of carrots that would have provided scant profit nor to selling large volumes of unsightly vegetables that would have undermined her reputation. Although she was successful in part because of the quality of her vegetables, she used her profits to buy land, trucks, and greenhouses (to produce food all winter long). Likewise, her attentiveness to the potentials and constraints of nature is manifest as the virtue of stewardship that reflects the mean between control and conciliation. She recognizes that she must work within constraints but that the land's productivity can be improved over its natural state by draining and other manipulations. Selina's attention to harmony and reciprocity is, in effect, a recipe for Aristotelian moderation.

However, it is too simple to suggest that ecofeminism merely recapitulates the Greek virtues. LaRocque's thoughtful critique not only contributes to a creative reframing of the virtues in ecofeminist terms but also provides a constructive break with classical philosophy. Like Des Esseintes, the Greeks were imbalanced in their focus on intellect and rationality (at least this is how they were understood by later Western philosophers). Ecofeminists do not reject reason; they simply and convincingly advocate balance. They call for us to be fully human by attending to all of our being—feeling as well as thinking. And they understand that there is a place for passion, that even moderation must be moderated. So it is that the "break" with tradition is, in a sense, really a deeper affirmation of that tradition.

The way in which ecofeminists would have us cultivate a virtuous life of mind, body, and soul would be in much the same way that Aristotle advocated—practice. A person must practice being generous, compassionate, empathetic, caring, and rational until these qualities become one's nature. Through such attentiveness we can avoid the ethical pitfalls of Des Esseintes and work toward *eudaimonia*.

CONCLUSION

If ecofeminism is an ironic philosophy, this suggests that it has elements of incoherence and depth. While all of us hold incoherent beliefs, we ought not aspire to incoherence. There is no inherent virtue—and even some cause for concern—when our values are in conflict with one another or our actions. But an element of inconsistency seems necessary to live and act in a world where ecological variation, perverse incentives, unintended consequences, moral luck, and humbling complexities abound. And it is in this sense that the ironies arising from the ecofeminists' view of literature might be understood. Perhaps the deepest insight in this regard comes not from a philosopher or literary critic but a writer. Barry Lopez (2001: 413) reminds us:

> No culture has yet solved the dilemma each has faced with the growth of a conscious mind: how to live a moral and compassionate existence when one is fully aware of the blood, the horror inherent in life, when one finds darkness not only in one's culture but within oneself? If there is a stage at which an individual life becomes truly adult, it must be when one grasps the irony in its unfolding and accepts responsibility for a life lived in the midst of such paradox. One must live in the middle of contradiction, because if all contradiction were eliminated at once life would collapse. There are simply no answers to some of the great pressing questions. You continue to live them out, making your life a worthy expression of leaning into the light.

Bibliography

Aay, Henry. 1993/1994. "Environmental Themes in Ecofiction: *In the Center of the Nation* and *Animal Dreams*." *Journal of Cultural Geography* 14, no. 2: 65–85.

Alaimo, Stacy. 2000. *Undomesticated Ground: Recasting Nature as Feminist Space*. Ithaca: Cornell University Press.

Allen, Paula Gunn. 1998. *Off the Reservation: Reflections of Boundary-Busting, Border-Crossing Loose Canons*. Boston: Beacon Press.

Anzaldúa, Gloria. 1987. *Borderlands/La Frontera: The New Mestiza*. San Francisco: Aunt Lute Books.

———, and AnaLouise Keating. 2000. *Interviews/Entrevistas*. New York: Routledge.

Armbruster, Karla. 1998. "'Buffalo Gals, Won't You Come Out Tonight': A Call for Boundary-Crossing in Ecofeminist Literary Criticism." In *Ecofeminist Literary Criticism: Theory, Interpretation, Pedagogy*, Eds. Greta Gaard and Patrick D. Murphy. Urbana: University of Illinois Press.

Arneil, Barbara. 1999. *Politics and Feminism*. Oxford: Blackwell.

Bacon, Francis. 1996a. *The New Organon. Collected Works of Francis Bacon*, Eds. James Spedding, Robert Leslie Ellis, and Douglas Denon Heath. Vol. IV. London: Routledge/Thoemmes Press. 37–248. Reprint 1875 ed.

———. 1996b. *Of The Dignity and Advancement of Learning. Collected Works of Francis Bacon*. Vol. IV. 273-498.

———. 1996c. *Of The Dignity and Advancement of Learning. Collected Works of Francis Bacon*. Vol. V. 3–119.

———. 1996d. *Sylva Sylvarum. Collected Works of Francis Bacon*. Vol.II. Pt. II. 331–680.

———. 1996e. *Valerius Terminus of The Interpretation of Nature. Collected Works of Francis Bacon*. V. III. Pt. I. 215–52.

Benjamin, Jessica. 1988. *The Bonds of Love: Psychoanalysis, Feminism, and the Problem of Domination*. New York: Pantheon.

Benjamin, Marina. 1993. "A Question of Identity." In *A Question of Identity: Women, Science, and Literature*, Ed. Marina Benjamin. New Brunswick, NJ: Rutgers University Press.

Bernheimer, Charles. 1997. *Figures of Ill Repute: Representing Prostitution in Nineteenth Century France*. Durham: Duke University Press.

Biehl, Janet. 1991. *Finding Our Way: Rethinking Ecofeminist Politics*. Montreal: Black Rose Books.

Bile, Jeffrey. 2011. "The Rhetorics of Critical Ecofeminism: Conceptual Connection and Reasoned Response." In *Ecofeminism and Rhetoric: Critical Perspectives on Sex, Technology, and Discourse*, Ed. Douglas A. Vakoch. New York: Berghahn Books.

Birkeland, Janis. 1993. "Ecofeminism: Linking Theory and Practice." In *Ecofeminism: Women, Animals, Nature*, Ed. Greta Gaard. Philadelphia: Temple University Press.

Bonta, Marcia Myers. 1991. *Women in the Field: America's Pioneering Women Naturalists.* College Station: Texas A & M University Press.

Botkin, Daniel B. 1990. *Discordant Harmonies: A New Ecology for the Twenty-first Century.* New York: Oxford University Press.

Bradford, Richard. 2001. *The Complete Critical Guide to John Milton.* London: Routledge.

Brooks, Paul. 2000. Foreword. In *And No Birds Sing: Rhetorical Analyses of Rachel Carson's Silent Spring*, Ed. Craig Waddell. Carbondale: Southern Illinois University Press.

Brown, Charles S. 2007. "An Introduction to the Problem of Boundaries in Ecological Theory and Practice." In *Nature's Edge: Boundary Explorations in Ecological Theory and Practice*, Eds. Charles S. Brown and Ted Toadvine. Albany, NY: State University of New York Press.

Buell, Lawrence. 2001. *Writing for an Endangered World: Literature, Culture, and Environment in the U.S. and Beyond.* Cambridge: Harvard University Press.

———. 2005. *The Future of Environmental Criticism: Environmental Crisis and Literary Imagination.* Malden, MA: Blackwell Publishing.

———, Ursula K. Heise, and Karen Thornber. 2011. "Literature and Environment." *Annual Review of Environment and Resources* 36: 417–40.

Butler, Gregory G. 1980. "Music and Rhetoric in Early Seventeenth-Century English Sources." *The Musical Quarterly* 66, no. 1: 60–62.

Campbell, Andrea, Ed. 2008. *New Directions in Ecofeminist Literary Criticism.* Newcastle, UK: Cambridge Scholars Publishing.

Carlassare, Elizabeth. 1999. "Essentialism in Ecofeminist Discourse." In *Ecology*, Ed. Carolyn Merchant. Amherst: Humanity Books.

Carr, Glynis, Ed. 2000. *New Essays in Ecofeminist Literary Criticism.* Cranbury, NJ: Associated University Presses.

Carson, Rachel. 1955. *The Edge of the Sea.* Boston: Houghton Mifflin.

———. 1962. *Silent Spring.* New York: Houghton Mifflin.

———. 1989 (1951). *The Sea Around Us.* New York: Oxford University Press.

———. 1992 (1941). *Under the Sea-Wind.* New York: Plume.

———. 2002 (1962). *Silent Spring.* New York: Mariner.

Chowdhury, Anupama. 2009. "Historicizing, Theorizing, and Contextualizing Feminism." *ICFAI Journal of English Studies* 4, no. 1: 28–39.

Clark, Suzanne. 1991. *Sentimental Modernism: Women Writers and the Revolution of the Word.* Bloomington: Indiana University Press.

Collard, Andrée. 1989. *Rape of the Wild: Man's Violence Against Animals and the Earth.* Bloomington: Indiana University Press.

Comer, Krista. 1999. *Landscapes of the New West: Gender and Geography in Contemporary Women's Writing.* Chapel Hill: University of North Carolina Press.

Conn, Sarah A. 1995. "When the Earth Hurts, Who Responds?" In *Ecopsychology: Restoring the Earth, Healing the Mind*, Eds. Theodore Roszak, Mary E. Gomes, and Allen D. Kanner. San Francisco: Sierra Club Books.

d'Eaubonne, François. 1974. "Le temps de l'écoféminisme." In *Le féminisme ou la mort.* Paris: Pierre Horay.

Descartes, Rene. 1960. *Discourse on Method* and *Meditations.* Trans. Laurence J. Lafleur. Indianapolis: Bobbs-Merrill Educational Publishing.

Dobson, Joanne. 1997. "Reclaiming Sentimental Literature." *American Literature* 69, no. 2 (June): 263–88.

Donovan, Josephine. 1998. "Ecofeminist Literary Criticism: Reading the Orange." In *Ecofeminist Literary Criticism: Theory, Interpretation, Pedagogy*, Eds. Greta Gaard and Patrick Murphy. Urbana: University of Illinois Press.

Eiseley, Loren. 1958. *Darwin's Century.* New York: Doubleday.

Eisler, Riane. 1990. "The Gaia Tradition and the Partnership Future: An Ecofeminist Manifesto." In *Reweaving the World: The Emergence of Ecofeminism*, Eds. Irene Diamond and Gloria Feman Orenstein. San Francisco: Sierra Club Books.

Emerson, Ralph Waldo. 1983 (1841). *Emerson: Essays and Lectures*. New York: Library of America.

Felski, Rita. 1991. "The Counterdiscourse of the Feminine in Three Texts by Wilde, Huysmans, and Sacher-Masoch." *PMLA* 106: 1094–1105.

———. 1995. *The Gender of Modernity*. Cambridge, MA: Harvard University Press.

Ferber, Edna. 1923. *So Big*. New York: Doubleday.

Friedman, Susan Stanford. 1998. *Mappings: Feminism and the Cultural Geographies of Encounter*. Princeton: Princeton University Press.

Gaard, Greta. 1993. "Living Interconnections with Animals and Nature." In *Ecofeminism: Women, Animals, Nature*, Ed. Greta Gaard. Philadelphia: Temple University Press.

———. 1998. *Ecological Politics: Ecofeminism and the Greens*. Philadelphia: Temple University Press.

———. 2010. "New Directions for Ecofeminism: Toward a More Feminist Ecocriticism." *Interdisciplinary Studies in Literature and Environment* 17, no. 4: 643–65.

———, and Patrick D. Murphy, Eds. 1998. *Ecofeminist Literary Criticism: Theory, Interpretation, Pedagogy*. Urbana, IL: University of Illinois Press.

Garrard, Greg. 2004. *Ecocriticism*. New York: Routledge.

Gartner, Carol B. 1983. *Rachel Carson*. New York: Ungar Publishing.

Gearhart, Sally Miller. 1979. *The Wanderground: Stories of the Hill Women*. Watertown: Persephone Press.

Glotfelty, Cheryll. 1996. "Introduction: Literary Studies in an Age of Environmental Crisis." In *The Ecocriticism Reader: Landmarks in Literary Ecology*, Eds. Cheryll Glotfelty and Harold Fromm. Athens, GA: University of Georgia Press.

———. 2000. "Cold War, *Silent Spring*: The Trope of War in Modern Environmentalism." In *And No Birds Sing: Rhetorical Analyses of Rachel Carson's* Silent Spring, Ed. Craig Waddell. Carbondale: Southern Illinois University Press.

Gould, Stephen Jay. 2003. *The Hedgehog, the Fox, and the Magister's Pox: Mending the Gap Between Science and the Humanities*. New York: Harmony Books.

Green, Nicholas. 1990. *The Spectacle of Nature: Landscape and Bourgeois Culture in Nineteenth-Century France*. Manchester: Manchester University Press.

Gruen, Lori. 1993. "Dismantling Oppression: An Analysis of the Connection Between Women and Animals." In *Ecofeminism: Women, Animals, Nature*, Ed. Greta Gaard. Philadelphia: Temple University Press.

Harris, Randy. 2000. "Other-Words in *Silent Spring*." In *And No Birds Sing: Rhetorical Analyses of Rachel Carson's* Silent Spring, Ed. Craig Waddell. Carbondale: Southern Illinois University Press.

Haydn, Joseph. n.d. *The Creation: An Oratorio*. Arranged by Vincent Novello. New York: G. Schirmer.

Hirsch, Marianne. 1989. *The Mother/Daughter Plot: Narrative, Psychoanalysis, Feminism*. Bloomington: Indiana University Press.

Hollander, John. 1961. *Untuning the Sky: Ideas of Music in English Poetry 1500–1700*. Princeton: Princeton University Press.

Horkheimer, Max. 2004. *Eclipse of Reason*. London: Continuum. Reprint 1947 ed.

Howard, June. 1983. "Widening the Dialogue on Feminist Science Fiction." In *Feminist Re-Visions: What Has Been and Might Be*, Eds. Vivian Patraka and Louise A. Tilly. Ann Arbor: University of Michigan Press.

Huysmans, J. K. 1969 (1884). *Against the Grain [A Rebours]*. New York: Dover.

Huyssen, Andreas. 1986. *After the Great Divide: Modernism, Mass Culture and Postmodernism*. Bloomington: Indiana University Press.

Hynes, H. Patricia. 1989. *The Recurring Silent Spring*. New York: Pergamon Press.

Irigaray, Luce. 1993. *Sexes and Genealogies*. Trans. Gillian C. Gill. New York: Columbia University Press.

Jacobs, Naomi. 2003. "Barbara Kingsolver's Anti-Western: 'Unraveling the Myths' in *Animal Dreams*." *Americana: The Journal of American Popular Culture (1900–present)*: 2, no. 2 (Fall). [no pagination].

Jezer, Marty. 1988. *Rachel Carson: Biologist and Author*. New York: Chelsea House.

Kheel, Marti. 1993. "From Heroic to Holistic Ethics: The Ecofeminist Challenge." In *Ecofeminism: Women, Animals, Nature*, Ed. Greta Gaard. Philadelphia: Temple University Press.

King, Ynestra. 1989. "The Ecology of Feminism and the Feminism of Ecology." In *Healing the Wounds: The Promise of Ecofeminism*, Ed. Judith Plant. Philadelphia: New Society Publishers.

Kingsolver, Barbara. 1990a. *Animal Dreams.* New York: Harper Perennial.

———. 1990b. "Serendipity and the Southwest: A Conversation with Barbara Kingsolver." *The Bloomsbury Review* (Nov-Dec.): 3+.

———. 2000. *Prodigal Summer.* New York: Harper.

Kolodny, Annette. 1975a. *The Lay of the Land: Metaphor as Experience and History in American Life and Letters.* Chapel Hill: University of North Carolina Press.

———. 1975b. "Some Notes on Defining a 'Feminist Literary Criticism.'" *Critical Inquiry* 2, no. 1 (Autumn): 75–92.

———. 1984. *The Land Before Her: Fantasy and Experience of the American Frontiers, 1630–1860.* Chapel Hill: University of North Carolina Press.

———. 2007 (1980). "Dancing through the Minefields: Some Observations on the Theory, Practice and Politics of a Feminist Literary Criticism." In *Feminist Literary Theory and Criticism*, Eds. Sandra M. Gilbert and Susan Gubar. New York: W. W. Norton.

Lahar, Stephanie. 1993. "Roots: Rejoining Natural and Social History." In *Ecofeminism: Women, Animals, Nature*, Ed. Greta Gaard. Philadelphia: Temple University Press.

Le Guin, Ursula K. 1985. *Always Coming Home.* Berkeley: University of California Press.

———. 1989. *Dancing at the Edge of the World: Thoughts on Words, Women, Places.* New York: Grove Press.

Leach, Melissa. 1994. *Rainforest Relations: Gender and Resource Use among the Mende of Gola, Sierra Leone.* London: Edinburgh University Press.

Lear, Linda. 1997. *Rachel Carson: Witness for Nature.* New York: Henry Holt.

Legler, Gretchen T. 1997. "Ecofeminist Literary Criticism." In *Ecofeminism: Women, Culture, Nature*, Eds. K. Warren and N. Erkal. Bloomington: Indiana University Press.

Leopold, Aldo. 1968 (1949). *A Sand County Almanac.* New York: Oxford University Press.

Levin, Margarita, and Michael Levin. 2001. "A Critique of Ecofeminism." In *Environmental Ethics: Readings in Theory and Application*, Ed. Louis Pojman. Belmont, CA: Wadsworth.

Lockwood, Jeffrey A. 2008. "Why the West Needs Mythic Cowboys." *High Country News*, 40 (June): 14–17.

———. 2011. "Unwrapping the Enigma of Ecofeminism: A Solution to the Illusion of Incoherence." In *Ecofeminism and Rhetoric: Critical Perspectives on Sex, Technology, and Discourse*, Ed. Douglas A. Vakoch. New York: Berghahn Books.

Lopez, Barry. 2001. *Arctic Dreams.* New York: Vintage.

Lutts, Ralph H. 1990. *The Nature Fakers: Wildlife, Science, and Sentiment.* Golden, CO: Fulcrum Publishing.

Mack, Maynard. 1950. "Introduction." *An Essay on Man. The Poems of Alexander Pope.* V. III. Pt. I, Ed. Maynard Mack. London: Routledge. Reprint 1993. xi–lxxx.

Mathews, Nieves. 1996. *Francis Bacon: The History of a Character Assassination.* New Haven: Yale University Press.

McCay, Mary A. 1993. *Rachel Carson.* New York: Twayne Publishers.

McClary, Susan. 2002. *Feminine Endings: Music, Gender, and Sexuality.* Minneapolis: University of Minnesota Press.

McDowell, Elizabeth J. 1992. "Power and Environmentalism in Recent Writings by Barbara Kingsolver, Ursula K. Le Guin, Alice Walker, and Terry Tempest Williams." MA Thesis. University of Oregon.

Mellor, Mary. 1997. *Feminism & Ecology.* New York: New York University Press.

Merchant, Carolyn. 1989. *The Death of Nature: Women, Ecology, and the Scientific Revolution.* San Francisco: HarperCollins.

———. 2003. *Reinventing Eden: The Fate of Nature in Western Culture.* New York: Routledge.

Mitchell, W. J. T. 2002. *Landscape and Power.* Chicago: University of Chicago Press.

Moore, Bryan L. 2008. *Ecology and Literature: Ecocentric Personification from Antiquity to the Twenty-first Century.* New York: Palgrave Macmillan.

Moser, Terri. 1999. *Silence of the Dispossessed: Restoring Voice to the 'Other' in Selected Twentieth-Century Novels.* Tempe: Arizona State University Press.

Murphy, Patrick D. 1991. "Ground, Pivot, Motion: Ecofeminist Theory, Dialogics, and Literary Practice." *Hypatia* 6, no. 1 (Spring): 146–61.

———. 1998. "'The Women Are Speaking': Contemporary Literature as Theoretical Critique." In *Ecofeminist Literary Criticism: Theory, Interpretation, Pedagogy*, Eds. Greta Gaard and Patrick D. Murphy. Urbana: University of Illinois Press.

———. 2000. *Farther Afield in the Study of Nature-Oriented Literature.* Charlottesville: University Press of Virginia.

Newman, Vicky. 1995. "Compelling Ties: Landscape, Community, and Sense of Place." *Peabody Journal of Education* (Summer): 105–118.

Noddings, Nel. 2003. *Caring: A Feminine Approach to Ethics and Moral Education.* Berkeley: University of California Press.

Norwood, Vera. 1993. *Made from this Earth: American Women and Nature.* Chapel Hill: University of North Carolina Press.

Oelschlaeger, Max. 1991. *The Idea of Wilderness.* New Haven: Yale University Press.

Ortner, Sherry B. 1974. "Is Female to Male as Nature is to Culture?" In *Readings in Ecology and Feminist Theology*, Eds. Mary Heather MacKinnon and Moni McIntyre. Kansas City: Sheed & Ward.

Perry, Donna. 1993. "Barbara Kingsolver." In *Backtalk: Women Writers Speak Out.* New Brunswick, NJ: Rutgers University Press.

Pierrot, Jean. 1981. *The Decadent Imagination, 1880–1900.* Trans. Derek Coltman. Chicago: University of Chicago Press.

Plant, Judith. 1990. "Searching for Common Ground: Ecofeminism and Bioregionalism." In *Reweaving the World: The Emergence of Ecofeminism*, Eds. Irene Diamond and Gloria Feman Orenstein. San Francisco: Sierra Club Books.

Plumwood, Val. 1991. "Nature, Self, and Gender: Feminism, Environmental Philosophy, and the Critique of Rationalism." *Hypatia* 6, no. 1 (Spring): 155–80.

———. 1993. *Feminism and the Mastery of Nature.* New York: Routledge.

———. 1997. "Androcentrism and Anthropocentrism: Parallels and Politics." In *Ecofeminism: Women, Culture, Nature*, Ed. Karen Warren. Bloomington: Indiana University Press.

Pope, Alexander. 1950. *An Essay on Man. The Poems of Alexander Pope.* V. III. Pt. I, Ed. Maynard Mack. London: Routledge. Reprint 1993.

Prentice, Susan. 1988. "Taking Sides: What's Wrong with Eco-Feminism?" *Women and Environments* 10 (Spring): 9–10.

Proctor, Robert N. 1995. *Cancer Wars: How Politics Shapes What We Know and Don't Know About Cancer.* New York: Basic Books.

Quinby, Lee. 1990. "Ecofeminism and the Politics of Resistance." In *Reweaving the World: The Emergence of Ecofeminism*, Eds. Irene Diamond and Gloria Feman Orenstein. San Francisco: Sierra Club Books.

Raglon, Rebecca. 1997. "Rachel Carson and Her Legacy." In *Natural Eloquence: Women Reinscribe Science*, Eds. Barbara T. Gates and Ann B. Shteir. Madison: University of Wisconsin Press.

Reiners, William A., and Jeffrey A. Lockwood. 2009. *Philosophical Foundations for the Practices of Ecology.* London: Cambridge University Press.

Rooney, Ellen, Ed. 2006. *The Cambridge Companion to Feminist Literary Theory.* Cambridge, UK: Cambridge University Press.

Rossiter, Margaret W. 1995. *Women Scientists in America: Before Affirmative Action, 1940–1972.* Baltimore: Johns Hopkins University Press.

Roszak, Theodore, Mary E. Gomes, and Allen D. Kanner, Eds. 1995. *Ecopsychology: Restoring the Earth, Healing the Mind.* San Francisco: Sierra Club Books.

Rubenstein, Roberta. 1996. "Homeric Resonances: Longing and Belonging in Barbara Kingsolver's *Animal Dreams.*" In *Homemaking: Women Writers and the Politics and Poetics of Home*, Eds. Catherine Wiley and Fiona R. Barnes. New York: Garland Publishing.

Ryan, Maureen. 1995. "Barbara Kingsolver's Lowfat Fiction." *Journal of American Culture* 18, no. 4 (Winter): 77–82.

Sandilands, Catriona. 1999. *The Good-Natured Feminist: Ecofeminism and the Quest for Democracy.* Minneapolis: University of Minnesota Press.

Shakespeare, William. 1998. *Hamlet,* Ed. G. R. Hibbard. Oxford: Oxford University Press.

Shelley, Mary. 1980. *The Letters of Mary Wollstonecraft Shelley.* V. 1, Ed. Betty T. Bennett. Baltimore: Johns Hopkins University Press.

———. 1995. *The Journals of Mary Shelley.* 1814–1844, Eds. Paula R. Feldman and Diana Scott-Kilvert. Baltimore: Johns Hopkins University Press.

———. 1996 (1826). *The Last Man. The Novels and Selected Works of Mary Shelley.* Vol. 4, Ed. Jane Blumberg with Nora Crook. London: William Pickering.

Shirk, Henrietta Nickels. 1997. "Technical Writer as EcoWriter: The Rhetorical Legacy of Rachel Carson." *Conference of College Teachers of English Studies* 62 (September): 86–92.

Showalter, Elaine. 1990. *Sexual Anarchy: Gender and Culture at the Fin-de-Siècle.* London: Virago.

Shutkin, William A. 2000. *The Land that Could Be: Environmentalism and Democracy in the Twenty-First Century.* Cambridge: Massachusetts Institute of Technology Press.

Slonczewski, Joan. 1986. *A Door Into Ocean.* New York: Orb.

———. 2001. "A Door Into Ocean, by Joan Slonczewski," biology.kenyon.edu/slonc/books/adoor_art/adoor_study.htm.

Spitzer, Leo. 1963. *Classical and Christian Ideas of World Harmony.* Baltimore: Johns Hopkins Press.

Spretnak, Charlene. 1990. "Ecofeminism: Our Roots and Flowering." In *Reweaving the World: The Emergence of Ecofeminism,* Eds. Irene Diamond and Gloria Feman Orenstein. San Francisco: Sierra Club Books.

Starhawk. 1989. "Feminist, Earth-based Spirituality and Ecofeminism." In *Healing the Wounds: The Promise of Ecofeminism,* Ed. Judith Plant. Philadelphia: New Society Publishers.

Steele, Meili. 1997. *Critical Confrontations: Literary Theories in Dialogue.* Columbia: University of South Carolina Press.

Stevenson, Sheryl. 2001. "Trauma and Memory in Kingsolver's *Animal Dreams.*" *Literature* 11, no. 4 (Feb): 327–50.

Stratton, Susan. 2001. "Intersubjectivity and Difference in Feminist Ecotopias." *FEMSPEC* 3, no. 1 (December), proquest.umi.com.ezproxy.fgcu.edu/pqdweb?did=506202831&sid=3&Fmt=3&clientId=8631&RQT=309&VName=PQD.

Sturgeon, Noël. 1997. Ecofeminist *Natures: Race, Gender, Feminist Theory, and Political Action.* New York: Routledge.

Sunstein, Emily W. 1989. *Mary Shelley: Romance and Reality.* Baltimore: Johns Hopkins University Press.

Swartz, Patti Capel. 1993. "'Saving Grace': Political and Environmental Issues and the Role of Connections in Barbara Kingsolver's *Animal Dreams.*" *Interdisciplinary Studies in Literature and Environment* 1, no. 1 (Spring): 65–79.

Trinh, T. Minh-Ha. 1991. *When the Moon Waxes Red: Representation, Gender, and Cultural Politics.* New York: Routledge.

Tuana, Nancy, Ed. 1989. *Feminism and Science.* Bloomington: Indiana University Press.

Vakoch, Douglas A. 2011. "Preface." In *Ecofeminism and Rhetoric: Critical Perspectives on Sex, Technology, and Discourse,* Ed. Douglas A. Vakoch. New York: Berghahn Books.

Vickers, Brian. 1968. *Francis Bacon and Renaissance Prose.* London: Cambridge University Press.

———. 1989. *Classical Rhetoric in English Poetry.* Carbondale: Southern Illinois University Press.

———. 1996. "Bacon and Rhetoric," In *The Cambridge Companion to Bacon,* Ed. Markku Peltonen. Cambridge: Cambridge University Press.

Waddell, Craig, Ed. 2000. *And No Birds Sing: Rhetorical Analyses of Rachel Carson's* Silent Spring. Carbondale: Southern Illinois University Press.

Warren, Karen J. 2000. *Ecofeminist Philosophy: A Western Perspective on What It Is and Why It Matters*. Lanham, MD: Rowman & Littlefield.
Watt, Ian. 1957. *The Rise of the Novel*. Berkeley: University of California Press.
Watts, Connie Sue. 1994. "Ecofeminist Themes in the Fiction of Barbara Kingsolver." MA Thesis. Arizona State University.
Webster, James. 2005. "The Sublime and the Pastoral in *The Creation* and *The Seasons*." In *The Cambridge Companion to Haydn*, Ed. Caryl Clark. Cambridge: Cambridge University Press.
Weir, David. 1995. *Decadence and the Making of Modernism*. Amherst: University of Massachusetts Press.
Werden, Douglas William. 2001. "Women Farmers in Early Twentieth Century American Fiction: Gates, Cather, Glasgow, Ferber, and Hurston." PhD Dissertation. Fordham University.
Willis, Gary. 1986. "Le Guin's *The Left Hand of Darkness*: The Weaving Together of Dualities." *Riverside Quarterly* 8, no. 1: 36–43.
Winnicott, D. W. 1971. "Transitional Objects and Transitional Phenomena." In *Playing and Reality*. London and New York: Havistock/Routledge.
Wolmark, Jenny. 1994. *Aliens and Others: Science Fiction, Feminism and Postmodernism*. Iowa City: University of Iowa Press.
Wright, Melissa. 2000. "Maquiladora Mestizas and a Feminist Border Politics: Revisiting Anzaldúa." In *Decentering the Center: Philosophy for a Multicultural, Postcolonial, and Feminist World*. Eds. Uma Narayan and Sandra Harding. Bloomington: Indiana University Press.

Index

About the Contributors

Vicky L. Adams graduated from Knox College with a BA in English/creative writing and was awarded the Scripps Prize for outstanding achievement in English. She completed a master's in English at Illinois State University with a creative thesis. She received a PhD in literature with a concentration in nineteenth- and twentieth-century British literature from the University of Alabama. She has presented papers at national and international conferences and published poetry in small press journals. Additionally Adams has worked as an adjunct English instructor and in academic libraries. Her research and writing projects include Romanticism, the Romantic and Victorian novel, ecocriticism, and literature and other arts. She is currently an independent scholar residing in Falls Church, Virginia.

Julie Bayless completed her BA in creative writing from San Francisco State University and her BFA in animation/illustration from San Jose State University. She is the founder and coordinator of East Bay Animators, as well as a member of the Society of Children's Book Writers and Illustrators. Her honors include the First Place ED Net Media Arts Award in Traditional Animation. Her personal film *Flowers for Sarah* has been screened at dozens of film festivals as part of the animated compilation *25 Ways to Die*. As a member of the Sims Online Division at Electronic Arts, Bayless designed and created new assets, user interfaces, animation, layout, and print collateral. As a freelance Flash animator and illustrator, she creates character designs, backgrounds, and animation, while also consulting on script-writing and sound design. Her clients include non-profit organizations such as Art in Action and the SETI Institute, as well as commercial and documentary projects (www.juliebayless.com).

Monique M. LaRocque graduated *summa cum laude* with a double major BA in international affairs/Spanish and modern languages (French and German) from the University of Maine. She completed an MA in French from the Middlebury College School in Paris, France, and an MA and PhD in comparative literature from Indiana University. Her research interests include naturalism, Decadence, ecofeminism, and ecocritical literary theory. She is currently executive director of Professional and Continuing Studies at the University of Southern Maine. LaRocque is a member of Phi Beta Kappa and is a strong supporter of the humanities in higher education. She is a commissioner of the University Professional and Continuing Education Association, as well as a member of the Sloan Consortium's *Journal of Asynchronous Learning Networks* Student Satisfaction Advisory Panel. La-Rocque also serves on the editorial board of *Summer Academe: A Journal of Higher Education.*

Jeffrey A. Lockwood earned a BS in biology from New Mexico Tech and a PhD in entomology from Louisiana State University. After twenty years as an insect ecologist at the University of Wyoming, he accepted a split appointment between the department of philosophy and the MFA program in creative writing. He has published three collections of environmental/spiritual essays: *Grasshopper Dreaming* (2002), *Prairie Soul* (2004), and *A Guest of the World* (2006). Lockwood has written for *Orion, Conservation Magazine, New York Times, Boston Globe,* and *London Times.* His books include *Locust: The Devastating Rise and Mysterious Disappearance of the Insect that Shaped the American Frontier* (2004), *Six-Legged Soldiers: Using Insects as Weapons of War* (2008), and *Philosophical Foundations for the Practices of Ecology* (2010). He has been honored with a Pushcart Prize, the John Burroughs award, and inclusion in the *Best American Science and Nature Writing.*

Richard M. Magee graduated from the University of California at Berkeley with a BA in English in 1990. He completed his MA in English at California Polytechnic State University at San Luis Obispo in 1994 before moving to Fordham University for his PhD, which he completed in 2002. He has taught English literature and composition at Fordham and the State University of New York. In 2003 Magee joined the faculty at Sacred Heart University in Fairfield, Connecticut, where he is now an associate professor. His research focuses on nineteenth-century American literature and ecological literature, and he is currently working on a book studying sentiment in American horror stories.

Eric C. Otto is associate professor of Environmental Humanities at Florida Gulf Coast University, where he coorganizes the biennial Humanities and

Sustainability Conference. He is the founding liaison for the professional affiliation between the Association for the Study of Literature and Environment (ASLE) and the Science Fiction Research Association (SFRA). Otto is the author of *Green Speculations: Science Fiction and Transformative Environmentalism* (2012), and with his colleague Andrew Wilkinson he has written a chapter titled "Harnessing Time Travel Narratives for Environmental Sustainability Education" for the book *Learning for Sustainability in Times of Accelerating Change* (2012). His ecocritical science fiction scholarship also includes "The Mars Trilogy and the Leopoldian Land Ethic" and "Science Fiction and Transformative Ecological Politics: Biocentric Wisdom in Three Early Works," as well as articles on environmental science fiction and Sally Miller Gearhart in *Women in Science Fiction and Fantasy* (2009).

Marnie M. Sullivan earned a BA in English with an emphasis in creative writing and a minor in chemistry from the University of Pittsburgh in 1991. Her interest in science and creative writing persisted as she earned an MA from Clarion University of Pennsylvania in 1993 with thesis projects that analyzed the use of science in *Star Trek: The Next Generation* and an excerpt from a novel. She earned a PhD in literature from Bowling Green State University in 2004 with a dissertation that examined Rachel Carson's three sea books from feminist and ecofeminist perspectives. Her research interests involve analysis of the creative expressions of traditionally underrepresented groups, literature of the environment, and science writing. Sullivan is a seasoned student advocate who has conducted research and presented papers on feminist pedagogy and service learning. She is currently a member of the English Department of Mercyhurst University.

Douglas A. Vakoch is professor of clinical psychology at the California Institute of Integral Studies, as well as director of Interstellar Message Composition at the SETI Institute. He is the general editor for Lexington Books' Ecocritical Theory and Practice series, as well as Springer's Space and Society series. Vakoch's books include *Ecofeminism and Rhetoric: Critical Perspectives on Sex, Technology, and Discourse* (2011), *Communication with Extraterrestrial Intelligence* (2011), *Civilizations Beyond Earth: Extraterrestrial Life and Society* (2011), *Psychology of Space Exploration: Contemporary Research in Historical Perspective* (2011), *On Orbit and Beyond: Psychological Perspectives on Human Spaceflight* (2012), *Astrobiology, History, and Society: Life Beyond Earth and the Impact of Discovery* (2013), *Altruism in Cross-Cultural Perspective* (2013), *Extraterrestrial Altruism: Evolution and Ethics in the Cosmos* (2014), and *Ecopsychology, Phenomenology, and the Environment: The Experience of Nature* (2014).

Theda Wrede is associate professor of English at Dixie State College of Utah. She teaches courses on U.S.-American ethnic literature, postcolonial literature, American cultural studies, and Western American literature. Her current research in these areas focuses specifically on the intersections of ecocriticism, gender, and ethnicity in the American West. Her book *The Way We Read James Dickey: Critical Approaches for the Twenty-First Century* (2009), coedited with William B. Thesing, was inspired by her editorial work on the *James Dickey Newsletter*. Her essays and reviews have appeared in the *South Atlantic Review, Interdisciplinary Humanities, Rocky Mountain Review,* and elsewhere. At Dixie State College, she is the chair of the undergraduate research program. Wrede has been a Fulbright scholar. She received her PhD in American literature from the University of South Carolina and her master's degree in English and French literature from the University Goettingen in Germany.